Hi-Fi

**Questions and Answers books are available
on the following subjects:**

Amateur Radio
Radio Repair
Radio and Television
Colour Television
Hi-Fi
Electronics
Integrated Circuits
Transistors
Brickwork and Blockwork
Carpentry and Joinery
Painting and Decorating
Plastering
Plumbing
Central Heating
Refrigeration
Automobile Brakes and Braking
Automobile Electrical Systems
Automobile Engines
Automobile Steering and Suspension
Automobile Transmission Systems
Car Body Care and Repair
Diesel Engines
Light Commercial Vehicles
Motor Cycles
Cycles and Cycling
Electricity
Electric Motors
Electric Wiring
Electric Arc Welding
Gas Welding and Cutting
Pipework and Pipe Welding
Lathework
GRP Boat Construction
Steel Boat Construction
Wooden Boat Construction
Yacht and Boat Design

QUESTIONS & ANSWERS

Hi-Fi

Clement Brown

Newnes Technical Books

Newnes Technical Books
is an imprint of the Butterworth Group
which has principal offices in
London, Sydney, Toronto, Wellington, Durban and Boston

First published 1974
Reprinted 1981

ISBN 0 408 00151 8

Printed in England by Butler & Tanner Ltd, Frome & London

Contents

PREFACE

This account of high fidelity sound reproduction is intended to guide amateur enthusiasts interested in serious listening and to serve more advanced students as a reminder of modern practice, the emphasis being on engineering aspects. It is hoped that the notes on principles underlying recent developments will convince readers that it is worth going to a certain amount of trouble to obtain better results.

An earlier book in this series on which this volume is based (*Questions and Answers on Audio*, now out of print) dealt with hi-fi practice as it was known at the time. Several innovations have attracted interest more recently, and this new account, embracing tape cassettes and noise-reduction methods, also reflects the sustained interest in high quality disc reproduction. The disc record has considerable potential and its importance must not be underestimated.

Emerging systems for surround sound provide a talking point for new and existing users of hi-fi equipment, and therefore a chapter on this subject offers a criticism and an account of recent developments. Stereophony is still in general use, however, and most of the discussion of electronics and transducers is based on twin-channel techniques.

All hi-fi sources are covered—discs, tapes and radio—and some guidance on costs, specifications and planning requirements is included. An increased variety of types of loudspeaker, a feature of hi-fi, is suggested by notes summarising activity in this field.

Certain illustrations have been provided by manufacturers named in the book, and their help is gratefully acknowledged.

C.B.

1

INTRODUCING HI-FI

What is meant by hi-fi?

The widely used label 'hi-fi' is an abbreviated form of 'high fidelity' sound. Unfortunately, despite some headway made with technical standards relating to specific types of sound equipment, there is no internationally acceptable definition of high fidelity. This lack of agreement has not prevented the gradual improvement of hi-fi systems, however, and it is arguable that the headway made in many areas of sound reproduction, much of it without benefit of any strong influence of work on technical standards, has in a competitive market been more rapid and brought greater gains than would otherwise have been the case.

Hi-fi is concerned with the faithfulness of recording, transmission and reproduction of sound. In fact it applies principally to the man-made links between the listener and the original sound, and is of most concern to those buying sound reproducing equipment for domestic use. It is reasonable to say that hi-fi represents an attempt to produce sound quality well above the average.

Clearly, any system of sound reproduction can convey a certain amount of information, and a cheap record player or radio can reproduce a reminder of the programme. Hi-fi goes well beyond basics and leads us to consider fidelity: we may seriously discuss it in terms of comparisons between the reproduced sound and the live or original sound. If the standard of realism is to be such that we can at least in some details compare the reproduction with the original, then it seems obvious that we should aim for the highest fidelity that is practicable—up to the limit imposed by the developing technology.

It is useful to note that the imprecise term 'hi-fi' is not universally liked; high quality reproduction is an obvious alternative. The idea of quality, however, does have a somewhat different meaning in a musical context, for voices and musical instruments have characteristic qualities and one orchestra will most certainly produce a better quality of sound than another. We should perhaps guard against any confusion that may arise when sound reproduction is discussed in music circles.

What is the purpose of hi-fi in practical terms?

There can be no confusion about the purpose of reproducing sound with a high degree of fidelity. The aim is to preserve the characteristics of the original, whatever its quality may have been. That is, the ideal high fidelity system is 'transparent' to its input, so that the original characteristics reach the listener unimpaired. Thus the output will enable the listener to judge whether the quality of the orchestra is good or bad, just as he could if seated in the auditorium.

If that conception of transparency is found acceptable, then it should not be difficult to assess any developments in audio engineering that appear to give the engineer or the listener some influence over the artistic aspects of sound reproduction. This is a point worth considering in view of the more exotic developments of recent times, references to which follow in later chapters.

Normally the programme producer and musical director take the artistic role and hand over their results to the engineer; influences on programme presentation would not be expected to extend beyond the studio and its output (the broadcast or magnetic tape). Further attempts to influence presentation, anywhere in the chain of transmission or reproduction, might appear to run counter to the achievement of fidelity to the original. Such attempts, however, are made from time to time and are bound to provide subjects for debate.

The development of sound equipment having a frequency bandwidth or response corresponding to the range of human hearing (that is, systems able to handle and reproduce the complete range of sounds, from highest to lowest, that it is possible to hear) is just one contribution to a state of affairs that produces transparency to a programme. Other factors are detailed in this book. In particular, the introduction of stereophony on a commercial scale enabled many more listeners to enjoy a higher standard of fidelity than was previously possible in domestic surroundings.

Indeed, standards have been, and are being, steadily raised, and much of the equipment which merited the description high fidelity a few years ago will no longer be acceptable now that there is a deeper understanding of techniques that influence musical results. Progress is more rapid in some areas than in others, of course, and certain kinds of loudspeaker system have changed very little during a period when quite considerable changes occurred in other, related fields.

When did hi-fi become important to ordinary listeners?

There have been improvements in the methods of transmitting and reproducing sound since the early days of radio and the gramophone, and better quality has been provided in response to demand. However, the last 25 years have seen the most important developments, including v.h.f./f.m. radio, tape recording and stereophony. Such developments have a longer history (stereo stems from nineteenth-century experiments) but widespread practical application has carried on the rapidly growing technology associated with the years following the second world war. It is certainly true that hi-fi as a hobby and a subject of study assumed great importance in post-war years when all sound reproduction was mono (monophonic) and plans for stereo had not reached commercial realisation.

What improvements have been made?

A particularly important advance, stereophony, is described later. For the moment it should be noted that this development cannot be fully appreciated unless it is allied to other, longer established techniques which have become part of good audio practice. An understanding of particular performance parameters was fostered by those responsible for high quality mono equipment, and it is true to say that good practice recognised many years ago is no less important when twin-channel techniques are applied. The same is true when we come to consider the latest multi-channel developments.

9

Among equipment developments of recent years is the almost universal use of transistors and other semiconductor devices together with printed circuits. This rapid change in the area of audio electronics does not necessarily have any great and direct bearing on the fidelity of reproduction but is seen to have some specific advantages. For example, amplifiers and receivers, although electronically more complex than they were a decade ago, can be more reliable and are certainly more compact. Some aspects of performance (f.m. radio, for instance) have rapidly improved with the availability of better, specialised solid-state components. There are reduced ventilation problems with transistorised units and, in some cases, power supplies are simplified.

Compact record/replay units for cassettes, suited to hi-fi systems, have become commonplace and owe much to solid-state developments. Transducers have been steadily developed and we can find worthwhile advances in pickups and loudspeakers. Reductions in the moving masses of pickup cartridges, together with control of distortions in these components, lead to a very noticeable gain in fidelity; and the refinement of loudspeaker systems, again yielding an audible advance, is associated with control of distortion and improved power handling capability, although some gains are at the expense of efficiency.

The ability of equipment to handle a wider frequency band is not especially attractive, and may even be shown to be undesirable, unless this is associated with very low distortion. Thus a feature of stereo pickup development is the attempt to control and reduce distortions arising in the tracing of the recorded modulations. Such distortions, militating against clarity, are highly objectionable in a wideband reproducer. The distortion in amplifiers has been steadily reduced, and a wide frequency response has been possible for many years.

At this point it is relevant to refer to the dynamic range of the recorded or transmitted sound (that is, the range from the quietest to the loudest sounds). Human hearing normally has to cope with a huge range in everyday sounds, and even in listening to live musical performances at a normal distance we experience a range of at least 70 dB (a ratio of intensities of ten million to one). A feature of development of recording and sound-reproduction systems has been an improved handling of dynamic range as a contribution to realism, and this implies better power handling and signal-to-noise ratios in the systems. A reproduced range of about 60 dB is a reasonable aim.

What are the main forms of distortion?

The main forms of distortion that may arise in the sound-reproduction system are: harmonic distortion, intermodulation distortion, transient distortion, frequency distortion, amplitude distortion and crossover distortion. Harmonic distortion is the generation within the system of harmonics of the original signal; intermodulation is the result of signals of different frequency inter-acting with each other to provide additional, spurious signals at the output; transient distortion, the inability of the equipment to respond to signals of very short duration (i.e. transients usually reaching a maximum value very quickly); frequency distortion is the result of inequalities in the equipment's sensitivity at different frequencies; amplitude distortion is the result of stronger signals not being amplified to the same extent as weaker signals; and crossover distortion is the result of the shape of a.c. signals being altered at the point where they change polarity. Also important is the signal-to-noise ratio, i.e. the proportions of wanted signal and unwanted background noise.

Adequate frequency response and reserve of power output take care of frequency and amplitude distortions. Crossover distortion is minimised or eliminated by correct design of the amplifier output stage (it should not be confused with untoward effects arising in 'crossover'—frequency dividing—filters in loudspeakers). More difficult to overcome are harmonic and intermodulation distortion, and it is usually figures for these that are given in hi-fi equipment specifications—especially in respect of amplifiers, for which methods of measurement are the best understood and longest established. Harmonic distortion in amplifiers can be kept to a fraction of a per cent (typically 0.08% in the mid-band at rated output). Similarly good transient response and signal-to-noise ratio result from careful design. Transient response is particularly relevant in the transducers, and big differences may be found between good and bad examples of such devices.

Further, with gramophone pickups there are tracing distortion, already mentioned, which is due to the fact that the reproducing stylus (hemispherically pointed or bi-radial) does not follow the recorded modulations (formed with a chisel-like cutting stylus) with complete accuracy; and tracking error, which is due to the deviation between the path that was travelled by the recording cutter, which moves in a straight radial line, and that followed by the pickup head which, on a conventional pivoted arm, moves in an arc across the disc. Tracing distortion is more serious than the effects of tracking error, for the latter are readily minimised by correct arm design.

What are the main features of a hi-fi system?

A complete system for the home would have all the components shown in Fig. 1. A stereo record player unit is assumed, and for

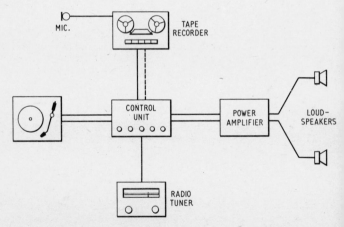

Fig. 1. Main components of a complete stereo system

most users the radio tuner also would be stereo. More widespread coverage by the BBC's v.h.f./f.m. service in stereo has led to a greater interest in receivers, high fidelity and otherwise. The tape recorder may be either a stereo or a mono machine. In practice only a

12

few people incorporate tape recording of the open-spool variety in fixed domestic systems. However, there is an accelerating interest in cassette machines.

The control unit incorporates tone controls and input-selection controls as well as preamplifier stages—essentially voltage amplifiers designed to accept low-level inputs and raise them to a high voltage level required to drive the power amplifier, which in turn develops the power to feed loudspeakers. In the majority of cases the control unit and power amplifier are combined to form an integrated unit, in one housing. Often the tuner is combined with the amplifier to form a receiver, otherwise called a tuner-amplifier. With increased opportunities to design compact equipment a further possibility arises—the complete system housing all the above items plus the turntable with pickup. A cassette section may also be included. However, the speakers are separate from the main unit or console.

How readily can hi-fi fit into the home?

Manufacturers pay considerable attention to the problems of making audio systems more acceptable. Ways have been sought to reduce bulk and improve design. To a great extent hi-fi requirements for loudspeakers are in conflict with the demand for compactness but there are some reasonably successful attempts to reduce speaker cabinet size while sacrificing as little as possible in performance. Such space-saving attempts become of even greater interest with the emergence of multi-channel systems. However, there is at the same time an upsurge of interest in high fidelity systems of the highest quality, a feature of which is the inevitably bulky, free-standing speaker of 'studio' or 'monitor' type.

Most hi-fi systems consist of separate units and it is usual to mount the various items on shelves, wall furniture or other supports. Loudspeakers can be mounted on walls if necessary, though the arrangement is inflexible.

What is the cost of hi-fi?

A very approximate range of cost of stereo systems is £100–800, assuming disc reproduction. Radio reception can be added for a minimum of around £40, and cassette facilities for £90–150 approximately. Systems of highest cost may be of professional calibre; those at the other end of the scale may incorporate some, but by no means all, of the hi-fi refinements.

Which factor has the biggest influence on sound quality?

Poor design or malfunction of any particular unit or component in an audio system could of course have a seriously detrimental effect on fidelity of reproduction. For instance, severe tracing distortion in record reproduction or abnormally poor transient response in a loudspeaker could spoil the performance of a system that might otherwise have some merits.

However, assuming an assembly of equipment of suitably high quality—'transparent' to the programme source as suggested earlier —it is the programme itself that finally determines the result. A disc record or a tape recording, for example, has in-built characteristics that determine whether a realistic representation of the music can be achieved. Important elements include recording balance, transmission of studio or hall acoustics (generally called 'ambience') and distortion present in the master recording.

It is often found that an outstandingly well engineered recording, while yielding its best via a high-grade audio system, will also sound unexpectedly pleasing on an inferior system. On the other hand, the superior system may well expose most critically the distortions and other deficiencies in a poor programme, demonstrating that, in general, advanced replay systems do not 'clean up' poor signals. Interesting exceptions are occasionally found in disc reproduction: certain types of mechanical shortcoming in discs, rendering them almost unplayable with cheap pickups, may not be very apparent when a high-grade pickup with superior groove-tracing capability is used.

It is reasonable to conclude that students of high fidelity sound reproduction should take at least as much interest in the technical quality of programmes as they do in the features of hi-fi equipment. Unfortunately there is plenty of evidence to suggest that very many users of equipment take this basic quality on trust, especially where LP discs are concerned. Although the quality of LP pressings is

14

frequently criticised and the quality control procedures of record manufacturers called into question, the underlying quality of recordings is less often given the close scrutiny it demands.

2

STEREOPHONIC SOUND

What is stereo and why was it introduced?

Stereophony can be described as a method of sound recording (or broadcasting) and reproduction aiming to produce in the mind of the listener an illusion that he is present in front of the original source of sound. In order to convey the information needed to produce this illusion, two or more separate channels of transmission—from sound source to listener—must be used. Monophonic (mono) sound transmission employs only one channel.

Although the mechanism by which the ears and brain estimate the source and direction of sounds is not perfectly understood, the work of many years on this subject did provide a basis for a new approach to sound recording and reproduction. The process whereby we locate sounds in the horizontal plane is evidently complex: at the lower frequencies it depends on the difference in arrival time or phase at the ears and at the higher frequencies it depends on the difference in arrival time and intensity. Interaural time/phase differences represent a very important factor.

In estimating the distance of sounds in the open air the brain relies on both memory and an assessment of loudness. In, say, a concert-hall the relationship between direct and reflected sound is important. Vertical localisation (elevation) involves head movements.

It is not possible to pursue such matters in this short account but reference must be made to the most important research and practical work, carried out in the U.K., which led to a stereo recording system. This work was started by A. D. Blumlein in 1929 and was preceded by various experiments in several countries. In Blumlein's system sounds are recorded in such a way that when they are reproduced by a two-channel reproducer the two loudspeakers are fed with signals of correct relative amplitude at all frequencies. The aim is to present at the ears of the listener the same resultant sound pressures as would have been heard at a corresponding position in front of the sound source. The innovation places some emphasis on positions of sound sources in the sonic image provided for the listener, although in more recent years other aspects of twin-channel reproduction have been accorded special attention.

A generally made assumption has been that information provided by reverberation in the recording is not influenced by the acoustics of the listening room, which is likely to have a short reverberation time. The recorded programme may reflect a reverberation time of, say, 1·5 s while a medium-sized room may have a mid-frequency reverberation time of 0·4 s. One might expect that the programme's reverberation (the 'ambience' quality) would seem to be overlaid on the room characteristics to some extent. For those unfamiliar with the term, reverberation time is the time taken for a sound to decay after cessation to one millionth (60 dB) of its original intensity. Reverberation is of course the echoing of a sound which gives an impression of persistence.

What are the main features of Blumlein's invention?

This work was based on the belief, supported by other investigators, that the difference in time of arrival of sounds at the two ears was the principal factor in source localisation. Therefore two microphones were placed close together; their phase differences were converted to amplitude differences and the resultant signals fed to two loudspeakers.

At first two pressure-sensitive (non-directional) microphones were used, and it was possible to modify their outputs to obtain amplitude differences. Later, two directional microphones were placed close together so as to be practically coincident: they were angled so that the polar characteristic gave the conversion to amplitude difference of the signals. A system of this kind found practical application in the U.K.

Fig. 2 shows the polar characteristic (i.e. looking down on the microphones) and it can be seen that a pair of figure-of-eight responses are combined. If the microphones are arranged to cover an orchestra or stage as in Fig. 3, the spread of sound reproduced via

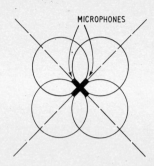

Fig. 2. Polar characteristics of coincident microphones

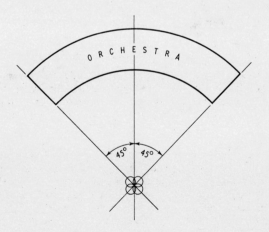

Fig. 3. Coincident microphones used to record an orchestra

Fig. 4. Technique shown in Fig. 3 results in a spread of sound during reproduction between the speakers

spaced loudspeakers as a laterally disposed image will be as shown in Fig. 4. This obvious outcome of the arrangement can be modified depending on circumstances in the recording studio.

Comment on other microphone arrangements for stereo.

The microphones may be spaced apart in various ways, instead of coincident, and the output from a single (mono) microphone can be

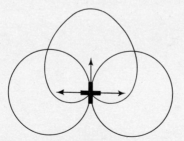

Fig. 5. Cardioid and bidirectional microphones are combined in the 'middle-side' recording system

part of the stereo mix. Also worth nothing is a configuration of German origin known as the middle-side system: in this a cardioid (directional) microphone, facing the performers, is combined with a bi-directional (figure-of-eight) microphone, as shown in Fig. 5.

Nowadays, however, the major companies commonly employ comparatively elaborate arrangements to give results far removed from those achieved by Blumlein and other early innovators. This is especially true of recordings of important musical works involving large orchestral and choral forces which are brought together in studios or halls where the most advanced and flexible equipment is installed. For a large symphonic work, say, or a performance involving a chorus and large orchestra, there would be a stereo microphone arrangement in front of the orchestra and other microphones with appropriate directional characteristics for certain individual performers such as players within the orchestra who are given important solos. Capacitor microphones with variable characteristics might be used in some instances. The percussion would have another microphone and possible additions would be non-directional microphones to the sides of the orchestra, their outputs being employed judiciously to heighten the 'ambience' effect, or impression of spaciousness, in the recording.

As many as 20 microphones, sometimes more, have been used for such sessions. Their outputs are mixed in the complex control equipment with which is associated a tape machine with 16 or more tracks. Final mixing and balancing involves an assessment of the characteristics and qualities contributed by the multi-channel input; and as a last stage the recording is reduced to two channels, reflecting the internal balance that was established in the studio and incorporating the detail that will, on reproduction, emerge in the stereo display between the loudspeakers. Mixing down to two channels is of course a necessary prelude to disc manufacture.

The ordinary listener may well feel that the various arrangements are of little more than academic interest. Whatever the principles employed, he will have to reproduce his records with one set of equipment and one arrangement of speakers. Moreover, discs rarely bear any indication of recording methods used. However, expert commentators often report on the subtleties of recording practice for the guidance of enthusiasts.

When did stereo first become a commercial proposition?

As far as British developments are concerned, the first commercially produced stereo discs were available in 1958. Stereo tape records (spooled tapes) had already been on the market for a short while but had made little impression.

Stemming from Blumlein's work, experimental stereo discs were produced in the U.K. in the 1930s. Other experiments involving the transmission of information through more than one channel (without a recording medium) were undertaken some time earlier. Indeed, a patent granted in 1881 described a system whereby telephone subscribers would receive relayed performances of opera and drama via headphones. Experiments with stereo radio were conducted in the 1920s in the U.S.A., Europe and the U.K.

From the evidence of these and other investigations it is reasonable to suppose that stereo would have been made available at an earlier stage it this had been practicable. Commercial exploitation had to wait, however, and it was because of the popular and familiar vinyl plastics LP disc that stereo found wide acceptance. At first the replay equipment was far from satisfactory but it soon improved. Within a few years some pickups gave a better performance than could be claimed for their mono counterparts.

Which principal gains are apparent to the listener?

Reference is often made, with every justification, to the sorting-out function of stereophony. The congestion that can easily be introduced in single-channel transmission of information is to a great extent overcome with two channels, which display the sonic detail in a lateral spread, or sound-stage. Good recording technique adds an impression of depth or perspective to this. Early over-enthusiastic claims concerning '3-D' tended to confuse the issue: stereo is certainly not three-dimensional, though it adds a dimension that is not present in mono.

The advantage of separation of sound sources within the stereo image is always apparent, making for better clarity and tonal quality (even single musical instruments are affected by this), provided the effects are contrived for properly musical reasons and without exaggeration. Associated with this separation is the presentation of inner detail; and there is a more convincing account of dynamic range, judged subjectively. Movement of sound sources is possible, whether this is contrived by panning the sounds across the image or allowed to occur naturally, as in some recordings of opera and drama.

Every bit as important is the attempt to convey the ambience or acoustical environment of the musical performance. The mixture of direct and indirect (reflected) sounds that is a normal part of the live listening experience can be picked up in stereo and to some extent presented in the front-located image set up between the loud-speakers. This may appeal as a fairly accurate account of the original sound or, as is common with some types of recording, it may be a simulation, dependent on artificial reverberation introduced electronically and judged by the recording producer to be appropriate to the performance.

Are there any means of producing artificial stereo?

Stereo requires at least two channels of transmission, and the results of modifying monophonic programmes cannot qualify as stereophony. Some experiments have been concerned with widening the apparent source obtained in mono reproduction. Attempts to delocalise mono sources, employing two or more speakers, include the use of electrical networks and acoustic delay devices to split the frequency band between spaced speakers, and the feeding of out-of-phase signals to two replay channels. These professional experiments are not relevant to the needs of the ordinary listener.

However, there are some cheap LP discs of reissued recordings, stemming from mono master tapes but described as 'electronically reprocessed' and claimed to give a stereo effect on two-channel reproducers. The originals in such cases were recorded before stereo was generally applied in the studios. It is evident that companies releasing these discs consider they will sell better if remastered with a stereo groove—rather than left in the mono, lateral-cut, state. A few novel effects are sometimes noticeable—a suggestion of de-localisation of sounds—but the discs remain essentially mono (as well as old), having nothing in common with modern stereo.

Can headphones be used for stereo ?

Yes, headphones are often used, especially for personal listening in circumstances where otherwise a disturbance might be caused. Strictly, headphones do not provide a stereo image: they are the termination of a binaural system in which one channel is isolated from the other at the listener's ears (Fig. 6). We may note that in his

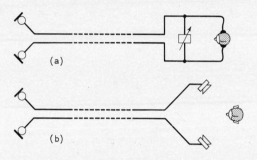

Fig. 6. (a) Binaural reproduction with addition of blend control. (b) Stereophonic reproduction

investigations Blumlein did not envisage the use of headphones (indeed, he specified loudspeakers), but certainly these devices will be found convenient and the better examples can yield a spacious-seeming and delicate quality of reproduction. Both dynamic (electromagnetic) and electrostatic transducers are in use. Some earpieces enclose the ears; others are of 'velocity' type, partly open-backed and imposing less isolation.

Can stereo include vertical as well as lateral information?

In his stereophonic experiments A. D. Blumlein considered the requirements for improving the stereo presentation and suggested ways of capturing vertical as well as horizontal information. He proposed (in 1931) using four or more speakers in arrangements that put one in mind of 'quadraphonic' developments. Such ideas

23

have not been realised in twin-channel stereo, but some suggestion of information in azimuth is conveyed by certain surround-sound experiments to which reference is made later.

How are two channels accommodated on a disc?

We should first refer briefly to the mono microgroove ($33\frac{1}{3}$ and 45 r.p.m. disc, as an introduction for the reader who is not very familiar with the gramophone. A lacquer blank is used, and a groove is formed in this by a cutter which moves laterally only. A cross-section of the groove is shown in Fig. 7a.

In tracing the modulated groove the stylus moves from side to side as in Fig. 7b, and this is the only movement needed for a single

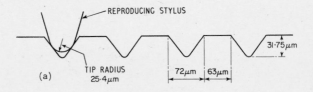

Fig. 7. (a) Record groove contour. (b) The reproducing stylus is moved laterally by the modulated groove

channel of information. The depth of the groove does not change. It is usual to speak of grooves, of course, although there is only one—a continuous spiral taking in the music grooves, the run-in groove, any intermediate banding grooves and the final run-off. On microgroove discs there are 150–300 turns to the inch. Most cutting lathes are

24

equipped with 'varigroove' facilities whereby the groove pitch can be varied, opening out when cutter excursions are great and closing again when the modulation is less severe.

In stereo recording, an unmodulated groove is the same as that on a mono disc. To accommodate two channels, a signal is cut on each groove wall: one is geometrically at 90 degrees to the other but at 45 degrees to the surface of the disc. This is known as the 45/45 system (see Fig. 8).

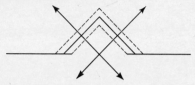

Fig. 8. The 45/45 system of stereo recording. A signal is cut on each wall of the groove

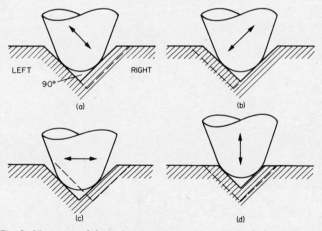

Fig. 9. Movement of the stylus in a stereo groove. (a) Right-hand channel modulated. (b) Left-hand channel modulated. (c) Both channels modulated equally and in phase. (d) Both channels modulated equally but in opposite phase

25

Directions of modulation and the movement of the replay stylus are depicted in Fig. 9. It can be seen that in-phase modulation (signals in step) produces lateral motion of the stylus, as in Fig. 9c, and that this is the same as mono. In a recording of any complex sound the stylus follows a variety of slanting, vertical and lateral movements which depend on the relative amplitudes and phase of the signals.

Whereas a stylus of 25μm (0·001 in.) tip radius is used to trace mono discs, a smaller tip is required for a stereo groove. The most usual size for a hemispherical tip in a high fidelity pickup is 12μm (0·0005 in.). However, the bi-radial or elliptical tip is most often used in the better grades of cartridge, and typical radii are 6 × 18μm (0·0025 × 0·0007 in.). Styli and pickups are described more fully later.

Can a stereo stylus be used to play mono discs?

A stereo pickup with a 12 μm (0·0005 in.) radius stylus tip can be used to play all microgroove discs, and it is sometimes found that the relatively small tip applied to mono grooves gives improved tracing of high-frequency modulations (though this depends on the condition of the discs). A compromise tip radius of 18 μm (0·0007 in.) can be used if necessary, but this is less often required now that so few mono discs remain in use.

A mono pickup must not be used to play stereo discs. Its stylus is designed for lateral motion and is stiff in the vertical direction. Therefore it is likely to damage the vertical component of the stereo modulation. A further point: a few music-lovers retain collections of 78 r.p.m. records and can arrange to use a separate cartridge fitted with the appropriate stylus for the larger groove. Note, however, that it is increasingly difficult to find a turntable equipped with the 78 r.p.m. speed.

Have other systems of stereo recording been devised?

Yes, but only the 45/45 system, already described, has reached commercial use on discs. In what is possibly the most interesting alternative, at one time the subject of experiments in the U.S.A. and the U.K., the sum of two channels was recorded as a normal mono recording, cut laterally in the usual way, and a frequency modulated carrier at about 25 kHz conveyed a signal representing the difference between the channels, as indicated in Fig. 10.

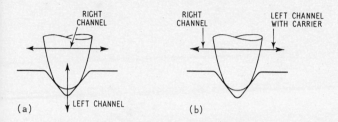

Fig. 10. Other systems of stereo recording. (a) *Vertical/lateral.* (b) *Frequency modulated (lateral) system*

For replay it was necessary to use a pickup with a very wide and smooth frequency response—linear to above the carrier frequency—but otherwise of normal mono design. Good results were reported but complex equipment was required to extract the twin-channel information. Since the recording was entirely lateral, the system was compatible with mono, and a mono pickup could be used to play the disc in the absence of equipment required for stereo reproduction.

Before the 45/45 system was adopted for general use, experimenters in the U.S.A., U.K. and Europe had investigated the 'vertical/lateral' system in which the groove was modulated vertically by the left channel and laterally by the right channel (see Fig. 10). It is of interest to note that Blumlein's invention had allowed for this alternative, and it is obvious that the system now used is the vertical/lateral system turned through 45 degrees. An earlier method involved two tracks side by side on a LP disc: this demanded a double pickup and two styli, and for obvious reasons it yielded a playing time of half that we now enjoy from LP records.

How are discs manufactured?

All recordings are of course made on magnetic tape. Recordings of various lengths can be made without interruptions, and tapes can be

27

edited as required. In some instances, particularly in the recording of classical music, tapes equivalent in length to a side of an LP disc may be recorded without a break. After the master tape has been completed, the main steps are: playback, with equalisation for the recording characteristic; cutting the lacquer master disc; production of positive and negative impressions by an electroplating process and of stampers (negatives) used for pressing the final discs; and lastly the mass production of discs in the factory. This sequence is shown in Fig. 11 and it applies to all kinds of discs, both 33 and 45 r.p.m.

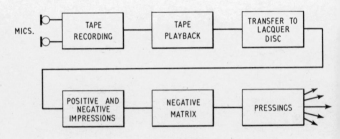

Fig. 11. Disc recording sequence, stereo or mono

The recording is transferred to the master disc—a smooth blank formed by coating an alloy core with a suitable lacquer—by feeding the disc recording head from a tape playback amplifier. This latter unit may have a power rating in the range 200 to 600 watts. In order to assist the formation of a uniform and noise-free groove the cutting stylus is heated to a temperature which will slightly soften the lacquer as cutting proceeds. The recording head with its chisel-edged stylus, formed on a piece of sapphire, simultaneously cuts and modulates the groove.

While the disc is being cut, the spacing between grooves is automatically adjusted so as to overcome the risk of the stylus cutting into an adjacent spiral of the groove during the recording of loud passages. This could happen because stylus movements are proportional to sound intensity. Elsewhere the spirals can be allowed to come very close together.

28

What is a recording characteristic?

It is the practice of varying in accordance with an accepted standard, called the characteristic, the level of the sound being recorded with respect to frequency. It is found necessary to attenuate the low-frequency signals because of the energy concentrated in the bass, and to emphasise the high-frequency signals in the interest of a good signal-to-noise ratio. The appropriate characteristic, displaying a response tilt from bass to treble, is obtained by means of electrical networks in the recording equipment.

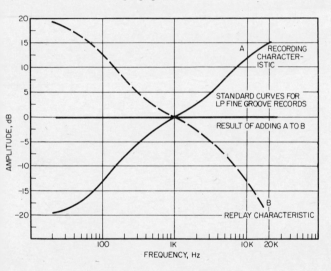

Fig. 12. Microgroove recording (A) and replay (B) characteristics. The replay characteristic is the inverse of the recording characteristic

The standard curve, shown in Fig. 12, is defined in British Standard BS 1928:1965. The illustration also shows the curve provided by a network in the hi-fi amplifier; since this is an inversion of the recording curve, the output of the network is a substantially 'flat' signal for subsequent amplification.

29

Is stereophony the basis for further improvement?

Stereo via discs and radio has been steadily refined, and the improvements have become evident to the hi-fi enthusiast particularly in respect of lower distortion, better detail in the stereo image, and a more convincing presentation of acoustical qualities—the ambience content of the twin-channel information mentioned earlier. Further investigation of recording methods has led to the emerging multi-channel recordings, which are explained in a later chapter.

However, there is a worthwhile possibility of deriving a simulated extra 'channel' from certain twin-channel records and broadcasts. Experiments have aimed at strengthening the impression of ambience surrounding the music and to some extent removing the emphasis from the front-located sound stage of stereo.

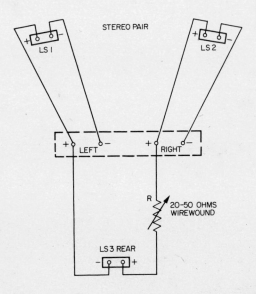

Fig. 13. Adding a rear speaker to an existing stereo system for a surround-sound effect. Level control (variable R) optional

30

This approach to what may be called 'surround-sound' relies on the fact that many recordings and some broadcasts have been found to contain concealed random information, normally part of the stereo image, that can be extracted for reproduction behind the listener, thus creating a better illusion of the direct and indirect (reflected) sounds which are a natural part of listening to music in an auditorium. The aim here is not to achieve marked directional effects, but rather to reproduce hall acoustics in a more imaginative way.

In this instance, since the information is to some extent already in the twin-channel disc or broadcast, conventional stereo hi-fi equipment is used for reproduction. The only extra items are one or two loudspeakers positioned experimentally behind or to the sides of the listener. The simplest method to expose masked ambience is to connect a rear speaker (see Fig. 13) provided the equipment is suitable for the imposition of an extra load in this way.

Out-of-phase components in the programme can be reproduced, all other components remaining part of the information reproduced by the front stereo pair of speakers. However, it is emphasised that results are not consistent, though they are obviously different from ordinary stereo with some proportion of commercial records. Some listeners have reported that success is achieved often enough to make this method an important one, at least while the merits of more complicated systems are being debated.

3

SURROUND SOUND

What are surround-sound systems?

This term is being applied to systems of recording and reproduction which go beyond stereophony as it has become established (i.e. twin-channel stereo with a pair of speakers), offering more directional effects and, hopefully, information about ambience and so on. Multi-channel systems are emerging, and large manufacturing organisations are competing for acceptance of their innovations, which so far are making little contribution to the progress of high fidelity and in any case are mutually incompatible.

Use of the term 'surround sound' does not imply the use of a particular number of channels in recording. The term 'quadraphony' has gained some currency, however, and to most people (and certainly to the record producers) this unfortunate word seems to incorporate proof that four channels are needed. To many, quadraphonic systems for replay must have four loudspeakers, although in fact there is no reason to suggest any connection between loudspeakers and the number of channels used.

Although an increase in the number of channels can have advantages, this has nothing whatever to do with the inputs to the system (which are numerous even with stereo), the number of tracks on the tape which inevitably is used for recording, or the number of outputs from the domestic system. If four speakers do in fact feature in hi-fi systems it is because that number is found to be the obvious solution for rooms of conventional shape.

Possibly the clearest thing about recent developments is that record-producing companies have accumulated a stock of four-track master tapes, mixed-down from studio tapes carrying 16, 24 or some other number of tracks. Aware that LPs are popular and familiar to all, the companies wish to transfer the recordings to a new kind of disc. Further, equipment manufacturers wish to sell more elaborate systems.

In what way is stereo inadequate?

At its best stereo can provide a pleasing and sometimes powerful reminder of what it is like to be present at the scene of the music-making. But no-one claims that stereo is the ultimate technique. Inevitably there must be attempts to produce a more convincing recreation of the subjective effects of being present where the music is performed.

Clearly, stereo can yield a front-located image in the form of a sound-stage with some suggestion of perspective and a great deal of detail accompanied by some ambience content, all mixed into the horizontal display. As now produced it gives no information about height. The way ahead involves reproduction of direct and reflected sounds in the right proportions, a mixture that is characteristic of the auditorium.

Improvement along these lines will be of value to the serious listener and is bound to be helpful if it can strengthen the illusion of being present where the performance takes place. Domestic reproduction of this calibre, allied to a high quality of sound (which in some ways has little to do with multi-channel developments) can fairly be said to support hi-fi objectives—that is, techniques which aid the pursuit of realism.

Examination of current recordings shows that the obvious differences between 'quadraphonic' reproduction and twin-speaker stereo are most enthusiastically exploited by pop-music producers; the characteristic presentation involves a number of pan-potted stereo images, set up between pairs of speakers, and an emphasis on unusual directional effects. Indeed, it is argued that pop music, having little reliance on accurate representation of live sounds (much of it exists by courtesy of audio technology), will make 'quadraphony' acceptable.

Unfortunately, the argument does not acknowledge that an ideal system, capable of reproducing ambience information and all the most ambitious directional and spatial effects, will embrace also the needs of pop music, drama, large-scale music and spectacular productions of all kinds. On the other hand, systems having superficial attractions in popular music have no technical merit for other programmes.

What terms are used to describe surround sound?

The terms gaining the most general currency have the least meaning. In particular, 'quadraphonic' (and 'quadrisonic', etc.) suggests a dependence on four but does nothing to explain what has happened in audio. The alternative 'tetraphonic' again suggests four but is hardly of greater merit since it does not reflect our objectives. 'Ambisonic' has been proposed and is better in that it suggests we are serious about ambience information. ('Ambiophony' is a linguistically inferior term sometimes used by manufacturers.)

Taking into account the properties of improved systems which have potential beyond that exhibited by quadraphonic four-speaker arrangements, the term 'periphonic' has been applied to a system capable of giving information in three directions, including height as well as horizontal direction; and 'pantophonic' has been suggested for a system which is ambisonic in the horizontal plane only. The latter has something in common with 'pan-potting', a term already mentioned in connection with the lateral spread of the stereo image.

What are the new recording systems?

There are several main contenders offering systems of encoding discs with the additional information needed for 'quadraphony'. The SQ (stereo-quadraphonic) system was devised by CBS in the U.S.A. and the QS system is a Japanese development due to Sansui. The latter is described as a matrix system ('matrix' is a jargon word used to express the idea of mixing signals), and there are some other Japanese and American matrix-type variants.

Whereas the above systems require fairly simple equipment for reproduction, including a conventional pickup of good quality capable of tracing the more complex groove modulations, there is another system which is technologically more advanced and demands more elaborate equipment for both recording and replay.

34

This is the CD-4 (compatible discrete 4-channel) system of the Japanese Victor Company (JVC). Domestic equipment must incorporate a wide-response pickup of special design and a demodulator, the latest versions of which employ integrated circuits.

Disc records exploiting the contending systems have been released commercially. For example, the SQ system has been adopted by EMI in the U.K. and is of course used by CBS also. The JVC CD-4 system has been adopted by RCA and the QS system by Pye. Problems of standardisation and international agreement are far from resolved; meanwhile some equipment manufacturers design hi-fi units in such a way that they can handle more than one type of record.

These competing commercial systems do not represent the only approaches. The UMX system devised by Duane Cooper of the University of Illinois and developed by Nippon Columbia, started with what is surely the right objective, which is to provide ambisonics by the simplest of means and to show how a further improvement follows from adding channels. Two, three and four-channel versions of the series are known as BMX, TMX and QMX. BMX is a two-channel phasor system with full mono compatibility; the base-band channels are encoded by simple sum and difference mixing, and any additional channels augment directional information and realism.

Since 1970 a U.K. project sponsored by the National Research Development Corporation has been conducted in association with the Department of Applied Physical Sciences at the University of Reading, England. Here again the aim has been to show that two channels can provide surround sound. This phasor system can be extended to employ extra channels to good effect. Since two major record companies and several minor ones remain uncommitted in this field at the time of writing, the claims made for new systems must be a matter of considerable interest.

What recording methods are used?

SQ uses a helical modulation method. Two channels are treated as in stereo using the 45/45 principle (see Chapter 2). Rear channels are modulated in a circular pattern, so that the groove walls impose a clockwise motion on the stylus for left-rear modulation and anti-clockwise for right-rear. In the QS matrix system all sound-image positioning is obtained from direction of stylus motion: horizontal movements produce centre-front information, vertical movements are centre-rear, and 45-degree motion corresponds to centre-sides (see Fig. 14).

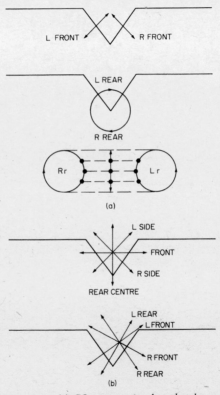

Fig. 14. Disc systems. (a) SQ system, signals and stylus motion. (b) Q system, signals and stylus motion

The above arrangements cannot really be called four-channel. Such non-multiplexed discs are strictly two-channel, though they have mixed-in information. In contrast, the CD-4 disc of JVC *is* a four-channel record. JVC confuse the matter by calling their disc 'discrete', evidently favouring this somewhat inappropriate word as a label to indicate separate channels. In fact a CD-4 disc is frequency-division multiplexed, incorporating base modulation plus further modulation on a carrier.

The groove is like that of the stereo 45/45-system disc, but two signals are recorded on both walls. One is the sum of the two channels and the other the frequency-modulated difference signal. The four-channel source signals are converted into sum and difference signals via suitable circuits; then the sum signals are cut in the same way as in twin-channel discs but the difference signals are

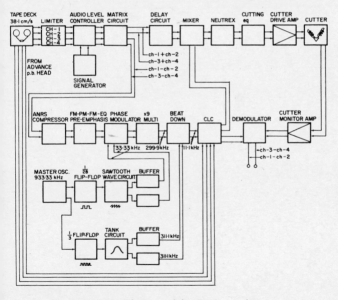

Fig. 15. Principal features of the CD-4 recording system

modulated, the carrier frequency being 30 kHz, and combined with the sum signals. The range lower than 800 Hz and higher than 6 kHz is frequency modulated and a range between 800 Hz and 6 kHz is phase modulated. On replay, equipment demodulates the difference signals and yields audio signals which are processed via matrix circuits to present separate outputs for amplification in the four-channel domestic system.

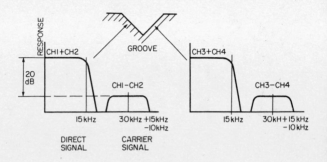

Fig. 16. Frequency response of the CD-4 system

CD-4 embraces a new disc-cutting method, a distortion-reduction process, an automatic noise-reduction system and the novel Shibata stylus shape for pickups. It is necessary for the pickup to track adequately up to about 45 kHz. Fig. 15 shows a schematic of the recording system and Fig. 16 illustrates the wide frequency response requirement.

What would be the features of an ideal system?

A system offering a substantial advance over stereo would give a much more realistic representation of direct and indirect sound mixtures—the ambience information to which reference has been made—and would produce a much improved illusion of concert-hall acoustics. Ability to pick out detail would be even better than it is with stereo; and at the same time the illusion of distance would be improved (this is much distorted in stereo). An impression of height

38

would be conveyed. Apparent dynamic range, sometimes referred to in connection with stereo, would be even wider.

Any system offering such attributes would be as useful for popular music, drama and spectacular effects as for the presentation of serious music in traditional styles. Unfortunately the emerging four-channel systems do not at present offer such features.

It should also be noted that systems employing fewer than four channels could provide what is needed: it has been found that a three-channel system can incorporate height information as well as ambience. Certainly it is true that a four-channel disc, such as the CD-4, could convey all that is needed, including information about height, although so far there has been no attempt to exploit the technology to such good effect.

How many units are needed for disc replay?

Commercial discs of the quadraphonic variety are intended for replay via four channels of reproduction, and therefore the first requirements are four amplification channels and four loudspeakers. Some commercially available audio systems include two large speakers for front positioning and two smaller speakers for use at the rear, but this arrangement appears to have been chosen for economy. Study of the properties of current recordings shows that four identical speakers should be used in systems where hi-fi performance rather than economy is the aim.

A replay system for discs of the SQ and QS types consists of a record player with stereo cartridge (this can trace all the encoded information in what is essentially a stereo groove), a decoder to produce four outputs, a four-channel amplifier and four speakers.

Equipment for CD-4 discs includes the special wide-band magnetic pickup cartridge, a demodulator producing four outputs and an amplifier and speakers as above. Domestic four-channel systems can reproduce stereo inputs, and it is claimed that the quadraphonic discs can be reproduced as stereo if required. However, it is very doubtful whether many stereo pickups could trace CD-4 grooves without to some extent damaging the high-frequency modulations.

It should be stressed that, as with stereo, four-channel replay could be at any level of quality. For hi-fi, the equipment should be of appropriate quality throughout—for instance, in respect of accurate groove-tracing, loudspeaker performance, power handling of the system, signal-to-noise ratio, distortion and so on.

Is the development limited to discs?

LP discs can perhaps make the programmes more acceptable, at least in the early stages, but four-channel cassettes have been developed and some open-spool tape records have been released in the U.S.A. and Japan. There have been experiments with four-channel radio transmissions.

4

DISC EQUIPMENT

What types of pickup are in general use ?

Pickups for stereo fall into two main categories—magnetic and piezo-electric. The first category, embracing many high fidelity models, includes moving-coil, moving-magnet and variable-reluctance pickups. In the second category are the crystal and ceramic pickups, the second of these types yielding the best performance. Lead zirconate titanate is one material that has been used for the piezo-electric elements, which generate a small voltage when subjected to bending or twisting.

A few alternative types have been developed but have not found wide application. These include strain-gauge, photo-electric and capacitance varieties. It is possible that there will be a revival of interest in such relatively unfamiliar principles of operation.

Pickups are commonly available in the form of 'cartridges'. This singularly inappropriate name is given to the actual transducer, which can be fitted into the head-shell of any pickup arm designed for this purpose. A few manufacturers have marketed pickup heads designed to fit particular arms, but at present nearly all hi-fi pickups are in cartridge form.

How do these pickups compare in cost and characteristics ?

A magnetic cartridge of advanced type is considerably superior to its counterpart in the ceramic range and costs several times as much. The benefits which follow from using a good magnetic cartridge in an arm of suitable quality include wider and smoother frequency response, lower distortion, more accurate tracing of transient information (often the most noticeable factor) and very slight, or negligible, wear of the groove. This last point is associated with control of mechanical impedance of the working elements and reduced tracking weight—the downward pressure on the groove. The most refined magnetic pickups excel in such respects.

Magnetic cartridges give less output than piezo-electric types and work into a smaller impedance. For example, a moving-magnet cartridge may generate only a few millivolts—a nominal 6 mV, say— and work into an amplifier input of 47 kilohms (a figure to which many designers work). A ceramic pickup generates many times this output voltage and requires an amplifier input impedance of about 2 megohms. A lower impedance adversely affects the bass response. Output and impedance figures mentioned here apply to each stereo channel.

These matters affect choice of amplifier. The same is true of the frequency response. The output of a magnetic pickup will correspond closely to the recording characteristics and therefore equalisation will have to be applied, as indicated in Chapter 2. This will normally be done in the amplifier.

The requirement is different for piezo-electric pickups. If the pickup is connected to an input of high impedance, as should be the case, it will itself approximately correct the response characteristic. Some amplifiers have a special input for this type of pickup and a few of the least costly units do not cater for any other type. However, most users of hi-fi systems prefer magnetic cartridges; this type is available in a wide price range; and the rapid development of transistorised amplifiers ensures that sensitive units, suitable for magnetic devices of low output, are available at prices to suit all users. Currently, magnetic cartridges are in the price range £5 to £60, and piezo-electric types rarely cost more than £5.

What are working principles of cartridges?

Variable-reluctance ('armature') cartridges are widely used (Fig. 17). The stylus bar or cantilever completes a magnetic circuit with each of the pole-pieces on which the coils are wound. In stereo variable-reluctance cartridges the poles are arranged so that flux due to one pair is at right angles to the flux from the other pair; movements of the cantilever, reflecting the motion of the stylus tip in the groove,

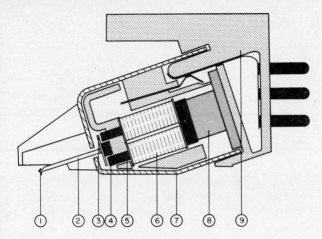

Fig. 17. Bang & Olufsen cartridge. 1, elliptical tip. 2, cantilever. 3, micro-cross armature. 4, suspension. 5, pole pieces. 6, coils. 7, mu-metal screen. 8, magnet. 9, bracket

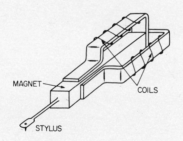

Fig. 18. Principle of the moving-magnet cartridge. The stylus is coupled to the magnet, and this assembly is pivoted so that the magnet moves within a magnetic circuit

change the lengths of the air gaps in the circuit. The magnet is fixed and the cantilever (armature) is of magnetic material.

In contrast, the moving-magnet cartridge (Fig. 18) has a small piece of magnetised material associated with the cantilever holding the stylus; this moves in relation to the pole-pieces, which are extensions of a magnetic assembly on which the coils are wound. This type was pioneered by Elac of Germany. Modern examples by Shure are particularly well known.

Of more recent development is the 'induced magnet' type. A small, fixed magnet, arranged close to the stylus assembly, induces a magnetic field in an armature forming an extension of the tubular, non-magnetic cantilever carrying the stylus tip. An obvious advantage is that the cantilever carries only an extremely small and light fragment of material, and the total mass of the moving system is very tiny. This principle is employed in cartridges by Goldring and A.D.C. The main components of an A.D.C. model are shown in Fig. 19.

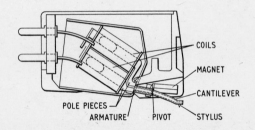

Fig. 19. Principal parts of the A.D.C. induced magnet cartridge

In the moving-coil cartridge, small and light coils are coupled to the stylus cantilever and move in a field created by a powerful fixed magnet. The output is usually very small, and for this reason—and to match the low-impedance coils to the amplifier—a step-up transformer or preamplifier is necessary. There are few cartridges of this type, but examples have been marketed by Ortofon, Micro Seiki and Sony.

In piezo-electric cartridges there are two ceramic or crystal elements. These can be clamped at one end and coupled to the stylus by means of a bridge of plastics material, as shown in Fig. 20a. The arrangement is such that a movement of the stylus will flex an

44

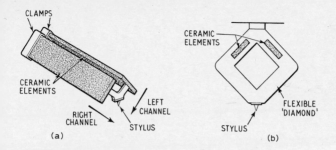

Fig. 20. Two forms of piezo-electric stereo cartridge: (a) *using a simple coupler for the stylus;* (b) *use of a diamond-shaped stylus coupler*

element. The coupling to the stylus can be completed by a flexible diamond-shaped structure as shown in Fig. 20b.

Cartridges suitable for 'quadraphonic' discs include existing hi-fi models and one or two specially developed devices. It seems likely that only magnetic types can qualify in respect of tracking ability and groove-wear. Cartridges for the CD-4 discs are magnetic devices with an unusually wide frequency response.

What are some typical specification points?

A magnetic cartridge of the more refined and costly kind will have a frequency response of about 20 Hz to 16 kHz. The upper limit is higher in a few instances. A small extension of the high-frequency response is not of great practical importance but smoothness of response in this region and elsewhere is essential for high fidelity applications. In fact several expensive cartridges exhibit a desirably flat response in the bass and mid-range and only a small departure (1 to 2 dB with respect to mid-range) in the treble.

The effect of mechanical resonances, suitably damped in any good pickup, should be small, but in any case the user must be sure he is not introducing resonances electrically, for instance by carelessness with terminating components and connecting leads. With practically all popular pickups the leads should be kept as short as possible, thus minimising the capacitance introduced in the amplifier input circuit. Fig. 21 shows a typical response after correction for the recording characteristic has been applied in the amplifier.

Crosstalk between channels in magnetic pickups will not usually be worse than 20 dB at 1 kHz (see Fig. 22). In any pickup there is an increase in crosstalk (i.e. a deterioration in separation of channels)

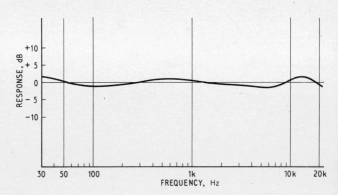

Fig. 21. Frequency response (one channel only) of a high quality magnetic pickup

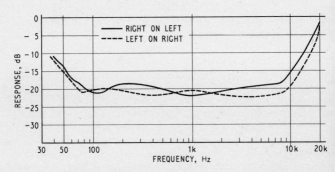

Fig. 22. Crosstalk of a high quality magnetic pickup

as the extremes of the audio range are approached. At the highest frequencies a rather sharp deterioration can be expected but this does not necessarily mean there is anything noticeably wrong about the reproduction. A close correspondence between channels in respect of output voltage and response is required and usually achieved.

For all types of pickup cartridge, tracking weights (permissible downward pressure) are gradually being reduced. This cannot be realised unless the mass of the pickup's moving system—stylus plus magnet, coil or armature—is also reduced. The mass in question is that which the groove modulation has to move. Again, this must be accompanied by a suitable increase in the moving system's compliance, which may be thought of as the 'give' or ease of movement at the pivot or other arrangement holding the stylus cantilever. However, this compliance should not be taken to be a direct indicator of the merit of a pickup: other factors are more important, and in any event an excessive compliance can be troublesome to the user, possibly imposing unwelcome restrictions on the choice of pickup arm to be used.

How low can the tracking weight be?

In general the tracking weight should be at the figure specified by the manufacturer of the cartridge. There may of course be a recommended range of pressures (typically 1–2 grams) for a cartridge which is suited to a variety of arms, and the minimum figure may well be practicable in only one or two arms of the highest quality. In any event the tracking weight must not be so low that the stylus does not ride correctly in the groove. Secure tracking demands proper contact between the groove and the stylus.

A reduction in tracking weight, associated with other refinements in design, is of course attempted in the interests of reduced groove wear and more accurate tracing of the impressed information. Some magnetic cartridges, used under carefully controlled conditions, can track average discs at less than one gram. However, this is possible only if the arm is of advanced design and properly installed and adjusted. In such conditions, groove wear can be practically eliminated—provided the grooves are kept clean.

The mass of the stylus and armature assembly has to be moved—and violently accelerated—by the recorded modulations. Very low figures—as little as a milligram—are quoted for the more expensive cartridges, but prospective purchasers should endeavour to ensure this figure really does refer to the effective mass acting at the tip of the stylus.

In recent times cartridges have been developed to track at around 0·5 gram but few have been considered suitable for general use. It is probable, however, that further work on commercial models will yield examples that are usable at such pressures, and their acceptance will inevitably depend on the availability of pickup arms that can give safe conditions of operation.

Why is an elliptical stylus used ?

This type of stylus has an approximately elliptical cross-section at the tip—where it actually contacts the groove. The elliptical, rather than the hemispherical, tip is now used in practically all of the more advanced hi-fi pickups and in some of the cheaper models. This is not a recent innovation, however, for elliptical styli were first made available many years ago for use on 78 r.p.m. discs.

Advantages are apparent in respect of information-tracing at high frequencies. There is an audible improvement in definition, and a gain in signal-to-noise ratio may be evident. Such advantages are not consistently realised on all records but generally the elliptical, or bi-radial, tip is worth its extra cost.

An improvement in the relationship between tip size and the high-frequency wavelengths in the groove might be expected from the use of a hemispherical tip of smaller than usual size (a 12·7 μm, 0·0005 in., tip radius has been regarded as customary). It has been demonstrated that a reduction to about 10·1 μm (0·0004 in.) radius can

Fig. 23. A stylus that is too small will ride too near the bottom of the groove

yield an improvement on some discs. But the proper point of contact is about half-way down the groove walls, and the stylus will introduce distortions if it rides too far down in the groove (see Fig. 23).

The elliptical tip offers a solution to the problem of maintaining proper contact between stylus and modulations at the correct position on the groove walls. It is supported correctly as seen from the front and rear; it has a smaller dimension in contact with the waveforms; and it provides a reduction in effective size as seen by the high-frequency modulations (see Fig. 24). It is not truly elliptical,

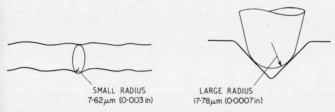

SMALL RADIUS
7·62 μm (0·003 in)

LARGE RADIUS
17·78 μm (0·0007 in)

Fig. 24. An elliptical tip fits short recorded wavelengths closely. Typical dimensions shown

but that is not a very important matter since any of a variety of shapes that come a little closer to the shape of the cutting stylus (without giving a cutting effect) is bound to offer greater accuracy of tracing.

A smaller area of groove-stylus contact will lead to accelerated wear (for a given downward force), and therefore the use of elliptical styli is associated with the downward trend of tracking weights. An elliptical tip with major and minor radii of about 17·78 μm (0·0007 in.) and 7·62 μm (0·0003 in.) is typical and quite widely employed, but the tracking weight should not be greater than about 1·5 grams if wear is to be acceptable. There are styli with larger radii for use in heavier tracking pickups.

Alternative stylus shapes have been advocated. One now gaining limited acceptance is the Shibata tip introduced by the Japanese Victor Company. Again it is an approach to cutting-tool shape and has a special feature, an increased area of contact with the groove and, at the same time, an improved relationship with the shortest wavelengths. Claims include longer tip life and improved signal-to-noise ratio. This innovation is associated with the development of 'quadraphonic' discs, but the tip shape has as much merit for the tracing of stereo discs.

What is the useful life of a stylus?

Local conditions, including pickup arm details and the state of the records, make an estimate of stylus life difficult. As a rough guide, assuming good conditions, an elliptical diamond tip may give 500–1000 hours of use (1500 to 3000 LP sides)—perhaps more in the care of a knowledgeable enthusiast. Some manufacturers can give estimates based on their own experience. Reported figures reflect differences between hemispherical and elliptical tips, the latter having the shortest life.

A fragment of diamond, accurately ground to shape and carefully polished, is the only satisfactory material for a stylus used in a high fidelity pickup. Other readily available materials wear rapidly or give a poor signal-to-noise ratio—or both. It is just possible that gradual improvements in pickups may open the way for the use of some alternative material which could be less hard and therefore easier to shape and polish. Certainly no change is imminent, and it may well be long delayed.

What are the main features of the pickup arm?

The role of the pickup arm is very simply described: it does not contribute to performance, but rather it provides conditions in which the cartridge or head can perform as the designer intended. Thus any obtrusive feature is unwelcome, and we can say that ideally the arm carries the cartridge smoothly and safely without introducing hazards or calling attention to its functions.

An arm should provide an adequate range of adjustment so that the pickup can be set-up for optimum performance. Simple consideration of mechanical engineering principles shows that the delicate and light modern cartridge will require an arm which has a small inertia while remaining durable and strong enough to withstand handling during the course of many years of use. If the pickup is to follow the small undulations and eccentricities naturally encountered during the tracking of a record, the pivots should introduce the least possible friction. The greater the pivot friction, the greater must be the downward pressure needed to keep the stylus in contact with the record groove, and clearly a condition of excessive friction is incompatible with efforts to decrease the tracking weights of cartridges.

As is well known a conventional pivoted arm is offset as shown in Fig. 25 and installed so that the stylus falls a little in front of the

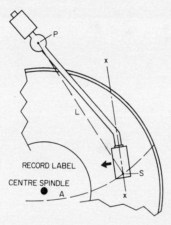

Fig. 25. Pickup geometry. Stylus S moves on an arc A as it traverses the disc. Axis X–X through the head is offset from the arm. L is effective length of arm. Friction of groove past stylus tip causes inward pull (bias) as shown by arrow, but this can be neutralised by outward correcting force

record centre. This is done to minimise tracking error. Although the axis through the cartridge or head is a tangent to the groove at only one or two points across the disc radius, correct design can ensure that distortion due to tracking error is slight at the minimum radius (60 mm, $2\frac{3}{8}$ in., radius is the standard observed).

With modern components this distortion can be very small and certainly less obtrusive than that introduced elsewhere in a system.

51

In practice an arm of 229 mm (9 in.) nominal length (stylus to pivot) may have an offset of about 23 degrees and a small stylus overhang, and the resulting tracking error is likely to be no more than ±1·5 degrees. Ideally the maximum error would be at the outside grooves of the disc. Final adjustment of a pickup should give zero error at the inner spiral of the groove, where distortion hazards are greatest.

Obviously the tracking error can be reduced by increasing the length of the arm. However, a long arm has greater inertia than a short arm, and this increase in mass is unwelcome in view of the trend to less massive cartridges. Elimination of the error is offered by a pickup that tracks radially, just like the cutting head that formed the groove. Such radial arms are coming into use but of course are more complicated and costly.

A radial arm traverses the disc without being subjected to any lateral forces. An ordinary pivoted arm, on the other hand, is subject to a small inward sidethrust due to the friction of the groove past the stylus and the geometry to which reference has been made. It is necessary to correct this effect in the interests of precise tracking at minimum downward pressure, and it is found that a simple device can exert a neutralising force—a small outward pull. Most arms for hi-fi use have such devices, usually of a mechanical nature (a suspended weight or lever device), but sometimes in magnetic form.

What are the general requirements for a turntable?

As with the pickup arm, the main requirement is dependable and unobtrusive service. Any really noticeable feature of operation is likely to prove a disadvantage, and in particular the introduction of audible interference, setting up a background noise, will militate against a good dynamic range by adversely affecting signal-to-noise ratio. Further, noise from the turntable (known as 'rumble') will mask detail in the reproduction.

Pitch fluctuations, due to small variations in turntable speed and known as wow and flutter, must also be reduced to an extremely small amount. Manufacturers appear to achieve success in this direction more easily than in improving signal/noise ratio. Wow is a slow fluctuation (below 10 Hz) and flutter is a fluctuation of higher periodicity.

A turntable that will give long-term performance to the standard required for high fidelity use, especially in respect of silent operation and superior speed constancy, is unlikely to be cheap. The cheaper kind of mass-produced unit, usually with some degree of automatic operation and often in the form of a record-changer, has poor characteristics and is totally unsuited to hi-fi use.

What are the main features of a 'transcription' turntable?

The term 'transcription', borrowed from professional practice, implies fine engineering and dependability. It has usually implied also a fairly massive construction, a notable feature being a very heavy turntable platter. However, it has become more difficult to categorise turntables in this way, and some modern units, though meeting the needs of hi-fi enthusiasts, are far less massive than the transcription turntables that have been popular among such users in the past.

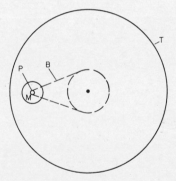

Fig. 26. Belt drive of turntable. A rubber belt transmits the drive from the motor pulley to a suitably dimensioned part of the turntable platter. The pulley can have two diameters and the belt can be moved from one to the other, selecting ratios for two-speed operation

Although some turntables, especially those incorporating complex mechanisms, are driven at the rim of the platter from a motor pulley via an intermediate idler wheel, the majority of relatively simple two-speed units (much favoured for hi-fi) have belt drive. A belt of rubber or a synthetic elastomer transmits drive from the motor to a suitably dimensioned section of the platter (Fig. 26).

As is well known, a large proportion of turntables have strobo-scopes, often with in-built illumination, together with provision for adjusting speed above and below the nominal speed. This arrange-ment enables the user to adjust the speed in relation to the mains frequency, which of course is applied to both the strobe and the motor. (For an absolute check on pitch a tuning fork could be used.)

It is evident that many listeners, using turntables with strobe devices, have their attention drawn to frequent, very small shifts in speed that would otherwise pass unnoticed; but it is of course important to correct large errors. One of the more recent innova-tions is the use of electronic speed control incorporating d.c. motor drive from a circuit in which corrections are made for any fluctuations in supply frequency (Fig. 27).

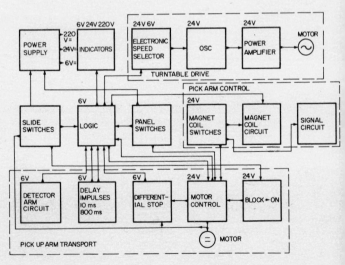

Fig. 27. Block schematic of the electronic elements in the Beogram 4000 turntable unit by Bang & Olufsen

54

5

HI-FI SYSTEMS

What are the important features of modern systems ?

Most modern audio systems of high performance are in unit form, as mentioned earlier. In a system of the most advanced kind all the units are purpose-built items, often from manufacturers with special experience of particular types of equipment. Those known for pickups rarely manufacture electronic products; turntable manufacturers are often specialists in appropriate branches of engineering; loudspeaker specialists seldom venture far into other areas, although there are a few outstanding exceptions.

Each unit should be chosen on its own merits but also with regard to the other units in the system. For example, with the knowledge that the favoured speakers are insensitive and destined for a large room and therefore will need plenty of driving power, the amplifier or receiver can be chosen partly on the basis of power rating but also with a view to the controls and other facilities required. Choice is seldom difficult: the variety is considerable and modern electronic units are versatile and flexible, so that problems need not arise if future addition of new auxiliary equipment is seen to be a possibility.

Questions of electrical matching in hi-fi systems are of a fairly simple kind and need not detain us. Most amplifiers cater for typical magnetic pickup inputs and some have two sets of inputs of differing sensitivity. Load terminations suited to popular pickups are normally provided, but any apparently large discrepancy should be investigated and corrected since a mismatch in this sense can affect the h.f. response on disc reproduction. Matching requirements for radio tuners, cassette units, etc., are readily visualised from reading the specifications.

Similarly, matching to loudspeaker loads is an obvious matter, and the worst of cases, possibly encountered by accident or carelessness, is one in which the load impedance falls too low for the particular amplifier. This may cause tripping of output circuit protection devices, the blowing of fuses, or unsatisfactory performance. This has occurred in instances where the amplifier was designed to deliver rated power into approximately 8 ohms but the speaker impedance fell to around 4 ohms in part of the range.

Should other aspects of matching be explored ?

There is another aspect of matching, more important than most other considerations yet not very obvious to inexperienced users of disc equipment. It is apparent that some systems, though having technical merit, do not prove satisfactory when judged subjectively. A flaw that is encountered all too frequently has to do with tonal characteristics, especially the mid-range and treble quality, and the actual details are not easily anticipated by the equipment buyer when he assesses the attractions of individual products.

Disappointment may stem from a lack of understanding that it is the transducers, rather than the electronic units, that influence details of sound quality most strongly. Typically, in a system that is otherwise of merit (having adequate power reserve, generally low distortion, etc.) response peakiness or the effects of poor mid-band tracking in the pickup may clash with an over-bright quality— perhaps a distortion peak or simply a response emphasis—in the loudspeakers. It is likely that such a characteristic would cause what is aptly termed 'listening fatigue'.

Clearly it is wise to investigate units and components to try to ensure that incompatibilities are avoided; and certainly the listener should interest himself in equipment auditions in order to gain an understanding of features of high fidelity performance. It is rewarding to check for overall smoothness and an unobtrusive yet well detailed quality.

Evidence of superior response to transients should be sought. The best results are to be expected from the most costly systems, but everything possible should be done to exclude the most severe incompatibilities in comparatively cheap equipment—where the effects of mistakes are bound to be the most hostile to musical realism.

Is the trend to high power ratings justified?

Very many modern loudspeakers of high quality are of low sensitivity and demand large inputs if they are to be driven (even only occasionally) to yield realistic sound levels. This is supported by typical figures quoted in Chapter 6. Indeed, it is found that several desirable attributes in speakers are gained at the expense of sensitivity, although figures quoted in respect of this parameter are no direct guide to quality.

Further, it is more widely appreciated that superior hi-fi performance, eminently satisfactory to the discerning listener by virtue of its unobtrusive quality and feeling of ease and refinement, lacks false emphases at high levels. A more coloured reproduction, marked by mid-range emphasis, may give greater subjective loudness and suggest a lower power requirement. The trend to higher outputs has been associated with overall improvement in quality, and the demand for ratings of 30–60 W or more has increased.

Although the popularity of low-powered systems has not been shaken by hi-fi developments, it is clear that such equipments are chosen because they are cheap, and not because there is any virtue in their modest ratings.

How can a decision be reached on power ratings?

A thorough investigation of requirements in individual cases would take many factors into account and prove unduly complex. However, it is widely regarded as satisfactory to relate power to conditions of use, making assumptions about the demands of the speakers if no specification figures are available to aid a closer estimate.

A particularly important requirement is a reserve of power, so gauged that output waveform clipping cannot occur under all likely conditions of drive; and this must also be established at a figure that ensures the speakers are driven to the sound pressure levels required. Obviously, power ratings for large rooms will be higher than for small rooms, other things being equal.

Local conditions must be borne in mind: it is necessary some-times to establish a wide dynamic range despite a high background or ambient noise level. The noise level determines the base of the dynamic range, and the power demand in the face of such local interference may be greater (by a factor of 6 dB or more, as a modest estimate) than for quiet conditions. It is for the user to decide whether or not to take such factors fully into account; it is likely that not many people explore this very seriously.

What guidelines should the beginner follow?

Experience of modern systems and popular taste leads to the follow-ing guidelines. Small, normally furnished rooms in which small speakers (nearly always of low sensitivity) are used will require amplifier ratings in the 10–20 W range. A rating of 10 W per channel leaves little if anything in reserve in any circumstances and in any case is appropriate to rooms of about 28–33 m³ (1000–1200 ft³).

It should be remembered that a doubling of this figure gives an increase of only 3 dB, reflected as only a small increase in subjective loudness. Ratings below 10 W cannot be seriously considered for hi-fi except where loudspeakers of unusually high sensitivity are available. Efficient horn speakers might provide the exception, but these are not very likely to be chosen for a small room.

A rating of about 30 W is required for a typical domestic lounge of 56 m³ (2000 ft³) and higher ratings are found necessary for larger rooms. The critical listener stands to gain from erring on the generous side, and 50–100 W ratings are currently used in no-compromise systems. Study of speaker power handling capability becomes especially important in this area.

The amplifier power ratings instanced here are continuous, sine-wave ratings; these usually appear in specifications of both British and imported amplifiers and should not be confused with 'music power' (an American novelty) or any other ratings based on simula-tion of programme inputs which may also be quoted but to which the sine-wave ratings bear no fixed relationship.

This question of ratings should not be left without reference to the basic incompatibility of speakers and amplifiers which is a feature of systems in which economies are made. Popular and inexpensive speakers are often insensitive, yet they are naturally used with types of amplifier least able to drive them to good effect. Possibly the worst combination is a low-powered amplifier and 'infinite baffle' speakers exhibiting an unfavourable impedance characteristic.

What form does the amplifier take?

An amplifier consists of two main sections, the control unit and the power amplifier, the first of these incorporating the preamplifier stages designed to handle signals at very low voltage levels. In practice the two main sections may be separate and linked only by electrical connections, but more often they are combined in one housing to form an integrated unit.

For stereo the controls may be separate for each channel but usually they are ganged (mechanically coupled) so that the controls function equally on each channel. If a separate control unit is preferred, this may be used with two single-channel power amplifiers or one stereo power amplifier, the latter being the most common solution.

What input arrangements are used?

Input sensitivities are particularly important. The sensitivity is the voltage required at the input to drive the amplifier to its rated output into a specified load. The smaller the voltage figure, the higher the sensitivity. Magnetic pickups are low-output devices and the input sensitivity to handle them is usually about 2 mV–5 mV. Typical input impedance at this point is about 47 kilohms (per channel). Having

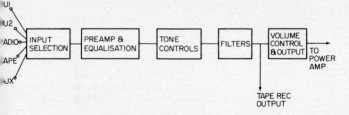

Fig. 28. Preamplifier section of a hi-fi amplifier

59

regard to the diversity of high-grade pickups, some manufacturers provide two such inputs of different sensitivities—typically 3 mV and 10 mV.

Ceramic pickups require lower input sensitivity but much higher impedance: 30 mV at 2 megohms is representative. However, ceramic and crystal pickups are little used for hi-fi nowadays, and very many amplifiers have no facilities for their connection. Such devices are used in some cheaper equipments, but the mode of connection is outside the scope of this book. Sensitivities in the region of 100–200 mV are appropriate for radio and tape units.

Inputs and the principal preamplifier and control stages are indicated in Fig. 28.

What arrangements are used for tone controls and filters?

Separate bass and treble controls are provided to enable the user to adjust the frequency response to suit his requirements. They are

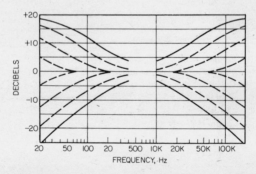

Fig. 29. Response curves obtained with Baxandall tone control system

often designed to give about 15 dB boost and cut (maximum) at, say, 50 Hz and 10 kHz relative to the mid-range. This is a substantial range of adjustment, and only a small part of it is likely to be used in systems of the highest quality. Indeed, it seems likely that such controls give an unnecessarily wide-ranging effect for many users.

The control system devised by Baxandall is designed to minimise distortion and to give reasonably sharp attenuation and boost at the extremes of the audio range. The response curves of this popular system are shown in Fig. 29.

Reference has already been made to ganged controls, the most usual arrangement. Dual-concentric controls, encountered in some high quality imported units, represent an alternative. The separate but concentric knobs can be turned together or independently. This method may be used for volume control as well as for the bass and treble. There are also some more complex tone control systems, particularly those publicised under the name 'sound effect amplifier' controls; at least five controls are used to adjust sections of the frequency spectrum—e.g. bass, upper bass, mid-range, upper-mid-range, treble.

High-pass filters are sometimes introduced to attenuate the lowest frequencies. Such 'rumble' filters, preferably switched, can lessen the effects of interference due to turntable rumble. However, one aim in

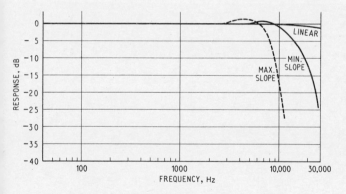

Fig. 30. Effect of a low-pass filter with variable attenuation

hi-fi reproduction is to achieve wide response associated with adequate dynamic range, and this can only be assured with a rumble-free turntable. Thus bass filtering within the audio range should not be necessary. However, there is a case for permanent

61

roll-off in the extreme bass (below about 20 Hz), as this can lessen ill-effects due to random noises.

A low-pass filter is intended to give a sharper attenuation of the treble than is possible with tone controls. It is useful when distortion, particularly objectionable at high frequencies, afflicts the programme. But clearly it is better to seek good programme material than to assume that filters are an inescapable feature of hi-fi.

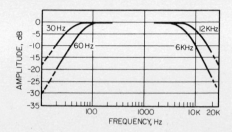

Fig. 31. Filter characteristics of Pioneer SA-1000 amplifier

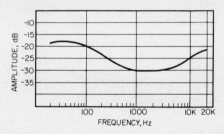

Fig. 32. Typical loudness contour, showing bass and treble lift relative to mid-range

The response curves of Fig. 30 show the effect of varying the slope, or rate of attenuation, of a low-pass filter—an additional refinement provided in a few amplifiers. The filter frequency here is about 8 kHz but the rate of attenuation can be varied within the limits shown.

In many commercial amplifiers the treble filter effectively duplicates the treble tone control function, thus adding to cost without serving a useful purpose. An exception is shown in Fig. 31, which depicts the treble and bass filter characteristics of a popular Japanese unit. Here, the two-stage filters give a rate of 12 dB per octave.

Loudness controls, emphasising the extremes of the range (relative to mid-range) for listening at low volume levels, are often encountered. The audible effect is often found to be extreme, and many users find it better to adjust the overall balance of sound by altering tone control settings if the reproduction is unacceptable at low levels. A typical loudness contour, checked with volume setting at − 30 dB relative to maximum rating, is shown in Fig. 32.

What is the balance control's function ?

This control enables the listener to centralise the stereo image. There may be differences between channels, arising electrically or in respect of the programme, and it is necessary to be able to adjust the volume of one channel relative to the other. In some instances the control provides only a small range of adjustment (a relative gain of 6 dB is probably adequate); in others there is complete fading of one channel with the control rotated to maximum. No balance control is needed if the amplifier has dual concentric volume controls, for these enable either channel to be adjusted over its full range.

What features do modern amplifiers have?

Higher power ratings have become popular in recent years, and figures of 15 W per channel (derived from continuous sine-wave measurements) are commonplace even for inexpensive units. The medium-power sector is about 25–40 W and amplifiers of higher power are in quite general use. Distortion has been reduced to the point where measurements are difficult, particularly when characteristics of measuring equipment give rise to concern. A total harmonic distortion as low as 0·03% is achieved. This figure relates to rated output of a 30 W amplifier, measured with 8-ohm test loads. Crossover distortion, arising from switching effects in output-stage transistors, has been virtually eliminated from high-grade amplifiers, although instances of it occur occasionally.

63

An interesting development, the subject of some controversy, is the use of direct coupling, without the familiar coupling capacitors, in circuits extending right through to the loudspeakers. This innovation is aided by the use of a split power supply having positive and negative outputs relative to ground. This is held to reduce low-frequency phase distortion and to be in the interests of a linear damping effect on the speakers—i.e. the source impedance of the output is kept to a very low value down to low frequencies. This implies a low-resistance supply source, to prevent malfunction in the event of the application of high-amplitude signals at low frequencies; hence the special attention to supply voltage regulation in some expensive units (a power supply for each stereo channel is the no-compromise solution).

There has been increased demand for multiple loudspeaker outlets on amplifiers. Typically, a hi-fi unit provides an arrangement whereby the user can switch between two or more pairs of outputs or employ these simultaneously, reproducing the programme in both the main listening room and other selected rooms. A greater emphasis on the dangers of overloading amplifier input stages has led to improved performance.

What causes input overload ?

Interest in this respect is focused on the input arrangements for pickups. A typical input sensitivity is 3 mV, and this may be viewed in relation to the nominal output of a magnetic pickup cartridge. Such a pickup will indeed generate about 3–5 mV at a specified recorded velocity (5 cm/s is the level usually quoted) but its output will be much greater at the peak recorded velocities which it is proper for hi-fi systems to embrace.

It is now more widely appreciated that very severe conditions are imposed by recent discs, and it is essential that amplifier input stages should handle the resulting peak voltages, which may be 40 mV or more. A 100 mV overload threshold (revealed by visible distortion of a test sine wave), for a nominal 3 mV input, is a reasonable requirement if adequate dynamic range is to be handled without subtle distortions and deleterious effects on transient response, and more amplifiers now meet such demands.

How is power response assessed?

It is, of course, of interest to investigate an amplifier's power delivery at frequencies other than 1 kHz (for which a figure may be quoted in the specification), and nowadays it is customary to measure 'half-power bandwidth'. This tells us the terminal frequencies where the power delivery has fallen by 3 dB (that is, half power) relative to the power at 1 kHz. A bandwidth of 25 Hz to 40 kHz is typical of a high quality amplifier, and some products yield a better result than this.

How can performance on transients be depicted?

Claims can be made for several methods of investigation and test-result display, though problems of interpretation sometimes arise. A commonly used method involves inspection of a square wave at a high or upper-mid frequency, with the amplifier driving into a test load consisting of 8 ohms resistance in parallel with a capacitance of, say, 1–2 μF.

Clearly, nothing would be learned from loading with pure resistance, as no hi-fi amplifier would be likely to reveal any deficiency

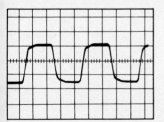 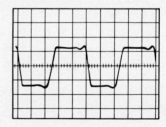

Fig. 33. Typical 10 kHz square-wave displays obtained with hi-fi amplifiers. Left: no overshoot on waveform. Right: well controlled overshoot

under this condition, and in any case practical use with loudspeakers imposes reactive loading of a somewhat unpredictable kind. The resistive/reactive test load causes amplifiers to overshoot slightly, and the extent of the 'ringing' and apparent degree of damping can be studied. Oscillograms from such a test are shown in Fig. 33.

How complex is a typical hi-fi amplifier?

The Armstrong 621 is a representative British-made stereo amplifier of acknowledged high quality, offering facilities likely to appeal to many users who demand a generous power rating yet cannot justify equipment of professional calibre. Some circuit features are shown in Figs. 34 and 35.

This manufacturer employs similar audio sections in integrated receivers (tuner-amplifiers) in the same series of products. In fact the series as a whole is based on 'modules' which are interchangeable between one model and another. Glass-fibre printed circuit boards are used. Output power is 40 W per channel into 8 ohms (continuous sine-wave rating) and 50 W into 4 ohms. Thus 4-ohm loading is permissible, although it is stipulated that the load must not fall below that value. Typical distortion is 0.06% at rated output in the mid-range.

Power supply features include a toroidal mains transformer (this construction permits compact unit layout with small height) and a bridge rectifier; a supply for the preamplifier section is obtained from a zener-diode stabilised regulator employing two transistors. A thermal delay in the supply section ensures slow charging of the reservoir electrolytic, much reducing switch-on thump, a noisy phenomenon noted in some amplifiers and one that many users find disturbing. There is some built-in attenuation of the extreme bass, plus switched filtering.

An unusual feature of this unit is source switching by diode gates (see Fig. 34). Each input has a diode in series with it, and selection of a source applies forward bias to the relevant diode, passing on the signal to the preamplifier. In the off condition there is no leakage through the diode; when on, the diode impedance is very small. The diode in operation feeds into an emitter-follower at high impedance. Another feature is the provision of low-level and high-level pickup conditions, selected by a switch, the highest sensitivity being 2.7 mV.

How is radio used in hi-fi systems?

Radio is an inexpensive audio source and is capable of excellent results. It is usual to associate a radio tuner, costing from about £30 to £100 or more, with a high fidelity amplifier. The alternative is to

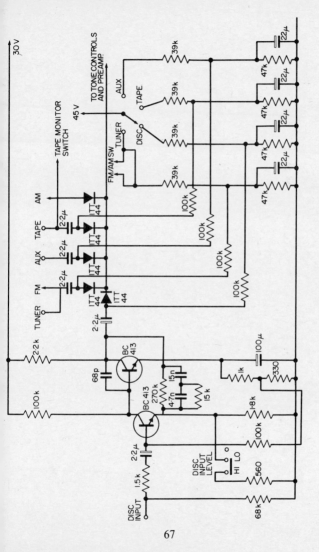

Fig. 34. Input stages of Armstrong 621 amplifier

67

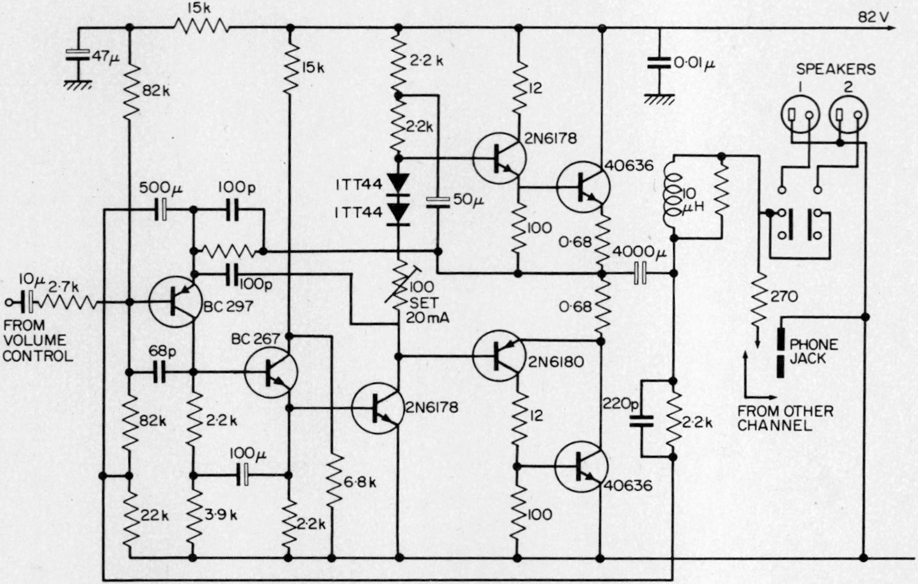

Fig. 35. Output stages of Armstrong 621 amplifier

68

install an integrated hi-fi receiver (i.e. tuner-amplifier), which incorporates a radio section and all the necessary audio facilities in one housing. Listeners who cannot receive v.h.f./f.m. can derive limited enjoyment from a.m. broadcasts (medium wave and long wave) but must accept the restricted frequency bandwidth and high noise and interference levels. However, f.m. coverage in the U.K. is now very general.

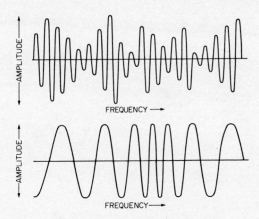

Fig. 36. Diagrammatic representation of amplitude modulation (above) and frequency modulation (below)

The fundamental difference between a.m. and f.m. concerns the way in which the transmitter's carrier wave is made to convey information. The two methods are compared in simple fashion in Fig. 36. In a.m. the carrier varies in amplitude in proportion to the audio signal which modulates it. In f.m. the carrier varies in frequency according to the audio signal, and the extent of the variation determines the audio amplitude. F.M. broadcasts are at very high frequencies (v.h.f.) and fall in the part of the v.h.f. band known as Band II, covering 87·5–100 MHz.

To the hi-fi enthusiast, a prime advantage of f.m. is the wide frequency response that can be reproduced, though results depend on what happens to the signal before it is transmitted. A response up to about 15 kHz is the aim but the use of land-lines to convey the programme from studio to transmitter often means that a narrower bandwidth is imposed.

The essentially noise-free nature of f.m. radio, however, is at least as important as the matter of response. It can be said that a small noise level spoils listening pleasure more than a small curtailment of bandwidth. The drawbacks of a.m. are only too familiar and need not be detailed here—interference and noise are of course prominent. Most types of interference are obviated in f.m. reception as long as the signal reaching the receiver is sufficiently strong. Unwanted amplitude modulation (e.g. local interference) can be removed by limiter circuits in an f.m. receiver or tuner.

Stereo broadcasting by v.h.f./f.m. has been steadily extended in the U.K. and the service is still being improved. The stereo multiplex system in use provides transmission that can be received as mono by ordinary f.m. sets such as the many portable receivers in current use. The sum and difference of the two channels are transmitted, only the former being received by mono sets. The difference signal is amplitude-modulated on a 38 kHz subcarrier; this is suppressed and the products of modulation are impressed on the main carrier by frequency modulation. A 19 kHz pilot carrier is transmitted as a synchronising signal, and this enables the subcarrier to be synchronised when it is reinserted at the receiver for stereo reception.

What is pulse-code modulation?

This is the latest innovation in f.m. broadcasting. The BBC now uses the pulse-code modulation system (p.c.m.) to link certain studios to the transmitters. This system offers important advantages compared with the old-established techniques but involves a new method whereby a signal is converted to a chain of pulses, subsequently identified and processed by a decoder. Audio information is converted to a series of digits corresponding to amplitude samples of the audio signal, for transmission via the p.c.m. link, and the method is less affected by noise and amplifying equipment non-linearity. Noise can be removed without affecting the quality of the digital information.

P.C.M. links are facilitating the extension of the stereo service. The first service for the several BBC networks was initiated in October 1972 and centred on London transmissions; extensions to the north of the country have been going ahead. A feature of the p.c.m. system is the high capacity: a single television channel can

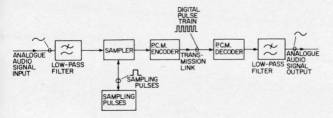

Fig. 37. Main elements of p.c.m. equipment at transmitter and receiver in the BBC system

embrace 13 audio channels. Encoded signals from 13 channels can be combined in a time-division multiplex arrangement permitting conveyance in a single circuit, the information bit-rate being 6·336 megabits per second. The basic idea of encoding and decoding is conveyed by Fig. 37.

Describe some performance features of a tuner

A stereo f.m. tuner intended for use in hi-fi systems of the most advanced type is the Marantz 115. This unit provides a.m. (medium-wave) coverage as well as f.m. As is usual, the switching from mono to stereo is automatic (i.e. the stereo decoder is activated with adequate signal) and when this occurs due to the presence of the pilot tone a stereo indicator illuminates.

Limiting on small signals is a feature of a high-grade tuner, and with this tuner a 30 dB signal-to-noise ratio is achieved with an input of only 1·2 µV. Distortion is about 0·3% for 100% modulation. Stereo switching occurred at about 12 µV. Adjacent-channel selectivity is 60 dB and capture ratio 1·5 dB. A.M. suppression is about 50 dB. This type of tuner is not only useful for reception of BBC stations when the listener is in the service area but can also provide practical reception of foreign f.m. broadcasts, given an appropriate aerial and favourable conditions.

Even a high-class tuner will not yield the expected performance unless proper attention is given to the aerial, and a cheaper unit certainly will not perform well without a generous input. An adequate signal is especially important for stereo reception. Although an indoor wire dipole is sometimes found acceptable in areas of high signal strength, it is generally necessary to install a properly designed dipole. This may sometimes be in the loft of a house, but an external aerial, mounted in a high position, is often desirable. Aerial manufacturers and local components suppliers are able to advise on types of dipole array likely to give best results. It cannot be too often emphasised that many complaints about f.m. reception arise because of neglect of aerial requirements.

6

LOUDSPEAKERS

What types of speaker system are available?

There are probably more loudspeakers on the market than any other component in the hi-fi chain. Undoubtedly this is due to the efforts of a large number of small companies equipped to assemble systems from parts which they themselves do not make. Many firms with an interest in audio, lacking resources or knowledge for work on electronic products, evidently feel qualified to enter loudspeaker manufacture.

The result is a great variety of systems, from shelf-mounted miniatures to massive free-standing models, of varying quality and spanning a price range of about £20 to £200 or more. The actual manufacture of the key components for many of these speakers is in the hands of the larger companies, some of which are responsible for innovations in this field.

Many working principles are involved. Speakers for hi-fi include 'infinite baffle' and vented systems, horns and labyrinths. Most systems are front-facing, having all the drive units arranged on a front baffle, but there has been some increase in the number of non-directional systems designed to give wide or general dispersion of output. The drive units in most systems employ electromagnetic principles (Fig. 38) but there are a few electrostatic transducers.

Published specifications are of limited value to the non-professional user, although they will of course reveal some features which are bound up with performance. But loudspeakers differ considerably in respect of total characteristics, and the prospective purchaser will search in vain, as things now stand, for a clear guide

73

to the qualities that may be aligned with his personal tastes. Specification figures or reports on speakers may lead the buyer to exclude unsuitable models from consideration and may even provide some information on the speaker's accuracy as a reproducer of signals applied to its input.

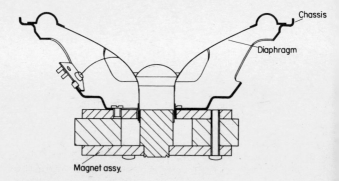

Fig. 38. Showing the principle of a modern 8 in. drive unit, the KEF B200

However, a decision about a particular example's suitability can only be made after careful listening. Since the properties of rooms affect the listener's impression of performance, the ideal arrangement is to make the decision after listening in the room in which the speaker is to be installed.

Optimum stereo can only be obtained with a well-matched pair of speakers. In this context matched means close correspondence of sensitivity, dispersion of output and frequency response in the upper part of the audio range.

How is the high frequency output extended?

A large diaphragm, as would be required for bass reproduction, does not respond well to high-frequency signals with their rapid, small-amplitude vibrations. A small, light diaphragm is necessary (see Fig. 39). Therefore multi-unit systems, in which the audio range is split up and handled by separate units of appropriate size, have

74

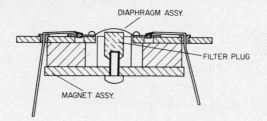

Fig. 39. Principle of a tweeter unit, the KEF T27

become popular. A well designed example will produce less inter-modulation distortion than a single unit, in which conflicting requirements are not readily satisfied.

Separate drive units may handle limited bands of low, middle and high frequencies; or one small unit may deal with inputs at frequencies above the point where the bass unit ceases to be an effective reproducer. This may be in the region of 1 kHz. In all instances the drive units are interconnected electrically by crossover filters.

Most of the smallest units, generally known as 'tweeters', are moving-coil devices. Some have cone diaphragms of plastics or moulded pulp, and others have a very small dome-shaped diaphragm of a tough and light plastics film. With this latter type it has been found possible to provide a smooth, extended response and good output dispersion. Some tweeters are in the form of pressure units in which a small diaphragm is coupled to the air with a horn to obtain sufficient output.

Ribbon and electrostatic units exhibit excellent response to transient signals. The former consists of a thin strip of metal foil suspended between the poles of a powerful magnet and coupled to the air with a horn. Electrostatic speakers are mentioned later.

How are crossover filters used?

The action of such filters depends on the frequency-discriminating properties of inductors and capacitors, these components being combined, with the possible addition of resistors, in suitable networks. However, the subject can be introduced by considering the simple addition of a tweeter to an existing speaker in order to reinforce the treble output.

Low-frequency input, which would damage the tweeter, is blocked by the capacitor, as shown in Fig. 40. The two units are in parallel and the capacitor is connected in one lead to the tweeter. This simple arrangement would hardly be suitable for a high quality system because the larger of the two units would not normally handle the entire range without some detrimental effect on the sound.

Where the frequency range is to be split between drive units, the filter consists of components as shown in Fig. 41, their values and

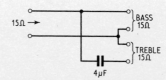

Fig. 40. Use of a capacitor to add a tweeter to an existing speaker in order to improve treble performance

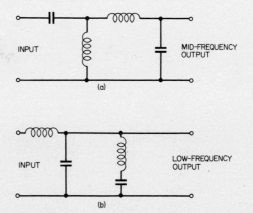

Fig. 41. Crossover filter sections. (a) Mid-pass section. (b) Low-pass section. These would be combined in a complete filter network

76

modes of connection determining the frequency of crossover and rate of attenuation of input to each unit. Enthusiasts devising their own circuits can obtain information from speaker manufacturers, some of which can also supply components and complete filters.

What is an 'infinite baffle' enclosure?

The term is applied to speaker systems which are more correctly called total-enclosure loudspeakers—a very popular type. Mounting a drive unit in the wall of a cabinet is of course a simple way to separate the outputs from front and back of the unit. Without the separation the outputs would cancel out at low frequencies. Apart from the use of a cabinet, a large cupboard or the wall between two rooms could serve as the mounting for a suitable drive unit.

Small total enclosures must involve a compromise where bass is concerned, but study of the behaviour of small systems has led to a variety of compact examples, some of them enclosing less than 0.028 m^3 (1 ft^3) of air and especially suitable for stereophony in small rooms, see Fig. 42.

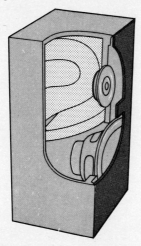

Fig. 42. Cutaway of typical IB system

In typical examples the bass unit has a freely suspended cone with very compliant surround and is designed to accept substantial input powers and to move as much air as possible. The main resonance of the unit is kept low in frequency (typically 25–30 Hz) since the frequency will be forced up due to the springiness of the enclosed air. The final system resonance may be in the 70–80 Hz region in a small infinite baffle loudspeaker. The response falls off fairly sharply below the system resonance but some compensation can be provided by driving more power into the system at low frequencies (by boosting the bass in the amplifier). Thus the system must be made to accept a reasonably large input without audible signs of distress.

The smaller types of total enclosure, or infinite baffle, system are very popular, but inevitably many buyers choose them because they are moderately priced and not for any special merits they possess. Indeed, the properties of many small speakers of good quality are in conflict with the requirements of users who assemble low-cost audio systems. In particular, a high quality 'bookshelf' speaker may be very inefficient, needing generous power input, yet it is likely to be chosen for use with an amplifier of low power yield—a choice dictated by a small budget.

What other types of system are used?

Commercial loudspeakers employing 'bass reflex' principles, horns and electrostatic transducers are encountered; so are systems of omnidirectional type and others which radiate output in particular ways.

The action of the bass reflex enclosure is based on the principle of the Helmholtz resonator: a volume of air inside an enclosure having a small aperture, or vent, is sensitive to a narrow band of frequencies when set into resonant vibration. In a simple example the main resonance is arranged to be at or near the bass resonance of the drive unit. When the enclosure resonance is the same as the reproduced frequency the cone meets a high acoustical impedance and its movement is damped; but the system is efficient at this point and produces output from the vent. Below this, the system's output falls off.

78

In some vented systems the aim is to produce optimum results from a particular unit in a relatively small enclosure, and the vent may be extended inwards to form a pipe. Fig. 43 shows one type of vented enclosure for a Tannoy drive unit and indicates the size needed for a 30 cm (12 in.) unit.

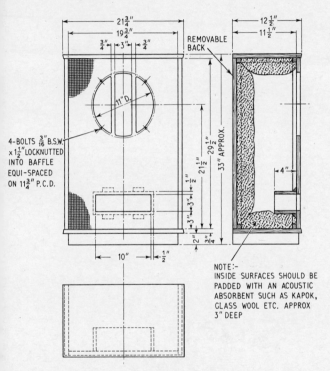

Fig. 43. Details of a Tannoy bass reflex enclosure design for a 12 in. dual concentric drive unit

A variant of this type is enjoying some vogue, at least for the time being. In a typical example the electrically driven bass unit is partnered by a passive unit—a suspended diaphragm without electrical connection—sometimes termed an 'auxiliary bass radiator' or 'drone'. At high frequencies this diaphragm simply behaves as part of the wall of the enclosure. Within a narrow band of low frequencies it is driven acoustically and comes into phase with the electro-acoustic bass unit, augmenting the bass output.

What is a 'monitor' loudspeaker?

The term 'monitor', correctly applied to loudspeakers that meet the requirements of professional users in recording and broadcast studios, has been applied in recent times to some high quality systems for domestic use. Professional requirements include high power handling capability and a dispersion of output suited to the conditions of use, allied to dependability. It is to be expected that most speakers meeting monitoring specifications will be bulky and expensive.

In view of the increased interest in audio equipment of virtually professional type for use in the home, it is not surprising that claims concerning 'monitor' quality have been made for a wider variety of loudspeakers. This is not always warranted, and some systems of domestic type, though of good quality, would not last long in the professional world before sustaining damage.

However, there are speakers that display the professional approach and can also be accepted in the home; low distortion, superior power handling and wide frequency response are notable characteristics. Another feature is transparency to the programme, and in this respect a few domestic monitors are better than systems that have become established in studios.

How is a horn used for domestic speaker systems?

A horn provides a highly efficient means of coupling a speaker cone to the surrounding air, but unfortunately a straight horn intended for bass reproduction is much too large for most homes! A straight horn may be used for high-frequency drive units: the wavelengths are small and effective coupling to the air can be achieved economically.

80

The horn is an 'acoustic transformer' matching the high mechanical impedance of the diaphragm to the resistance of the air, and therein lies the reason for its efficiency. A wide-range system can be accommodated if the horn is folded, and this results in a cabinet of acceptable dimensions in several commercial examples. If the drive unit is front-facing it can be rear-loaded by the horn and will radiate treble in the usual way. If necessary the horn-loaded unit can deal with the lower end of the range in a multiple system.

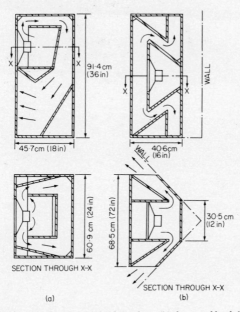

Fig. 44. Folded horn enclosures: (a) *back loading;* (b) *front and back loading of the drive unit*

Fig. 44 shows some possible arrangements—simple rear-loading of the drive unit and the application of the horn to both front and rear radiations.

What are omnidirectional speakers?

With this type the aim is to disperse the output as widely as possible. Mid-range and high-frequency output reaches the listener via nearby reflecting surfaces—walls, ceiling and other objects in the room—rather than directly into the listening area. In some commercial examples the output is projected upwards and sideways; the bass can in any case be regarded as non-directional. An arrangement of this sort makes the loudspeaker room-dependent and its performance unpredictable. There are also a few examples in which the output is partly direct and partly dependent on reflections.

Principal claims made for this type of speaker appear to be invalid, at least as far as stereo reproduction is concerned. It is said that stereo realism can be improved and that the impression of ambience overlaying the music can be heightened. This could be so only if information due to the use of two channels was improved in quantity and accuracy. But demonstrably the stereophonic information in the programme is confused by omnidirectional presentation.

Clearly, the ambience content is conveyed by a recording or broadcast, not by loudspeakers, and the requirement is to reveal this as accurately as possible. A room-dependent system, adding a mass of reflected sound, must be in conflict with this requirement.

What is an electrostatic loudspeaker?

This type consists of a rigid, perforated metal plate and a very light metallic diaphragm (or a film of suitably treated plastics). The diaphragm is held under tension and separated from the plate by a small air space. A varying voltage applied to the two parts causes corresponding movements of the diaphragm.

To reduce distortion it is necessary first to apply a fixed d.c. polarising voltage to attract the diaphragm to the metal plate by a certain amount; the signal voltages then vary this permanent attraction. Nevertheless this simple arrangement generated too much distortion for serious use.

Practical speakers of this capacitive type have a 'push-pull' arrangement in which the diaphragm is held between two perforated plates as shown in Fig. 45. The diaphragm can be of flexible plastics, coated with a thin metallic layer. One terminal of the polarising

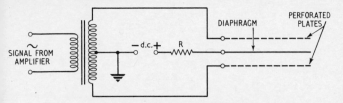

Fig. 45. Elements of a push-pull electrostatic speaker

supply is connected to the diaphragm through a high resistance R, which prevents variations of the electric charge during the time taken for large diaphragm movements. Indeed, a principal design aim is to ensure that large movements, needed for bass reproduction, can occur with a minimum of distortion.

The output from the amplifier is fed via a transformer with a centre-tapped secondary to the two perforated plates. The resulting speaker has a relatively linear response, and the small moving mass makes for superior performance on transient signals. With a big enough diaphragm, bass can be radiated without an enclosure. The only commercial example in the U.K. capable of wide-range reproduction is the Acoustical Quad.

A speaker of this kind, radiating to front and rear but not sideways, is known as a doublet. (An ordinary moving-coil cone speaker mounted on a flat baffle is similar in this particular respect.) A few small electrostatic radiators, such as that by B & W Electronics, are in use as mid-range and treble reproducers.

Are other complex systems used?

A number of commercial designs depend on the properties of a long pipe or duct, which is folded so as to occupy a reasonable amount of space. The labyrinth enclosure is of this kind. In a practical labyrinth (Fig. 46) the rear of the drive unit is loaded with a folded pipe which is a quarter-wavelength long at the lowest frequency to be reproduced. Thus for a limit of 50 Hz the pipe would be 1·68 m (5·5 ft) long. The end of the pipe is left open and the walls are lined with wadding. Back-radiation is dissipated by friction and absorption. Radiation from the end of the pipe is in phase with that from the drive unit cone, and at the quarter-wavelength a high impedance is imposed on the cone, damping it and minimising distortion.

Related to the labyrinth is the 'transmission-line' system in which the duct is tapered and energy is progressively dissipated. The term

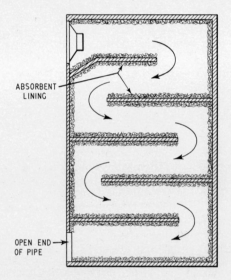

ABSORBENT
LINING

OPEN END
OF PIPE

Fig. 46. Labyrinth loudspeaker enclosure

'transmission line' seems to be derived from electrical technology and is not perhaps specially appropriate to acoustics, but it has become fashionable in the last few years. Extended, low-distortion bass response is possible with systems of this kind: a response to below 20 Hz has been achieved in systems of acceptable dimensions.

What loudspeaker specifications are there?

Specifications describe principles of operation, enclosure dimensions, types of drive unit and their crossover arrangements, and overall frequency range, to which may be added a frequency response with benefit of data on maximum departures from linearity of response under specified conditions. Harmonic distortion figures are sometimes included (though difficult for many users to interpret): typical figures are 1–2% at the lowest frequencies, with improvement higher in the range, quoted with reference to a particular sound pressure level (SPL).

It has become more common to quote a sensitivity figure. As an example: 11 W into nominal 8 ohms gives 96 dB SPL at 400 Hz, 1 m from the speaker in anechoic conditions (that is, in an anechoic test chamber). The 96 dB figure is derived from a sound pressure of 12 μbar, which has found some measure of international agreement. To obtain an idea of driving requirements, calculate the input to produce some higher SPL involved in reproduction of peaks of sound in a large space, remembering that an increase of 3 dB is a doubling of power. As a simple example, it can be seen from the above that 22 W will produce 99 dB SPL and 44 W 102 dB.

Rated power is often given as a maximum figure for programme input. A rating of 30–60 W is typical of a medium-sized speaker system. A maximum programme input appears to be the most useful to the ordinary user of hi-fi equipment, and added information concerning recommended amplifier power requirements provides guidance and reassurance for those planning complete audio systems. Several manufacturers quote such a recommended driving-power range—for example, 15 to 40 W. In that case, 40 W would be maximum programme input; it could not be expected that the speaker would yield realistic sound levels if driven by an amplifier rated below 15 W.

The nominal impedance (e.g. 8 ohms) is always quoted, but a complete account includes a graphical display of the impedance characteristic, showing departures through the range of operation. Finally, some users have reason to connect speaker systems in parallel, but before doing so they should consider the effect of the load thus presented to the amplifier. For instance, two 15-ohm systems might be connected to an amplifier suited to half that impedance (a nominal 8 ohms, say). Two 8-ohm speakers should not be connected in parallel without first obtaining confirmation that the amplifier can operate into the resulting load. Loudspeakers for hi-fi should not be connected in series.

7

TAPE EQUIPMENT

How widely is tape used in domestic hi-fi?

Although magnetic tape offers some notable advantages in the recording and reproduction of sound, open-spool tapes have featured infrequently in domestic systems. The objections of the non-technical user and music lover concern inconvenience and high cost. On the other hand, the technical matters causing problems for the general user are precisely those which attract many amateur enthusiasts and experimenters, who are prepared to exploit the obvious versatility of the medium.

Tape offers an especially attractive hobby, the pursuit of which does not necessarily involve the recording of music. The modern portable recorder is widely used in this way. Tape is of course always used professionally for music recording, and it forms the first stage in commercial recording prior to disc production. Direct-cut master discs are sometimes produced, and in such instances the programme is recorded without the intervention of tape, but in practically all large-scale disc production there is a master tape stage as described earlier.

The last few years have seen a rapid improvement in the quality of performance achieved with cassettes of tape, and cassette devices together with new types of record/replay machine are becoming more widely accepted in hi-fi circles.

What are the basic principles of recording?

Important electrical parts of the recording and replay system are shown in simplified form in Fig. 47. In this example separate amplifiers and heads are employed for recording and replay. Audio signals from the source (microphone, radio tuner, etc.) are amplified and fed to the electromagnetic recording head, which sets up an alternating flux. The tape, drawn past the poles of the head at constant speed, becomes permanently magnetised, the microscopic particles on the plastics-based tape taking up a pattern in accordance with the applied modulation.

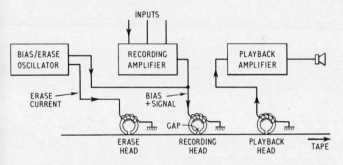

Fig. 47. Basic elements of a tape recorder. Record and replay heads are combined in many commercial machines

During recording, a bias signal derived from an oscillator working at a frequency well above the audio range, is also applied to the head in order to reduce the distortion which would otherwise arise in such a system. The oscillator also supplies the current needed to erase recordings from the tape.

To play back the recording the tape is drawn at the recording speed past the poles of the playback head, producing variations in flux and therefore of voltage in the head coil. The signal, at a very low voltage level, is amplified and its frequency response characteristic is modified. Two electrically separate channels of the kind outlined here are required for stereo.

In most of the more advanced recorders there are separate recording and replay heads as indicated in Fig. 47. In most popular-priced machines, however, a combined record/replay head gives a cost saving. A combined head is indicated in the tape deck layout of Fig. 48.

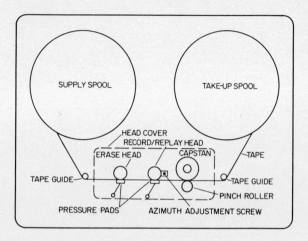

Fig. 48. Layout of a typical tape deck

The main task of the components on the deck is to move the tape past the heads at constant speed and under uniform tension. The tape is driven along by a capstan and held under pressure at this point by a suitable pinch-wheel (rubber-tyred roller). The capstan drive includes a flywheel to minimise speed fluctuations.

Which tape speeds are used?

High-frequency response depends on such factors as tape speed and head gap-width. Given a particular design of head the user will choose from the standard speeds according to the type of programme involved, remembering that with many open-spool machines it is still necessary to run at 19·05 cm/s ($7\frac{1}{2}$ i.p.s.) to ensure adequate extension of response. The 9·53 cm/s ($3\frac{3}{4}$ i.p.s.) speed is sometimes adequate for music recording if the machine is a good one, and speech is recorded at either 9·53 cm/s ($3\frac{3}{4}$ i.p.s.) or 4·76 cm/s

($1\frac{7}{8}$ i.p.s.). Speeds higher than 19·05 cm/s ($7\frac{1}{2}$ i.p.s.) are used professionally but for the amateur user they are uneconomic. Cassetted tape runs at 4·76 cm/s ($1\frac{7}{8}$ i.p.s.), as described later in this chapter.

Which tape materials are used?

Ferric oxide has been the principal tape coating material for many years and is still the subject of improvement. Chromium dioxide has been introduced recently, particularly for cassettes; there are also cobalt-doped materials and a new type of iron-particle tape has been developed. All such innovations are of special interest to the hi-fi enthusiast.

Tape manufacture involves two main processes, the production of the base film material and the coating process. The base material is usually either p.v.c. or a polyester such as Mylar. The latter is more stable in relation to temperature and humidity changes. Production is in wide rolls of considerable length, cut after the coating has been applied. Base materials may now be as thin as 18 μm and rigorous quality control is necessary, not least in respect of surface finish and variations in thickness.

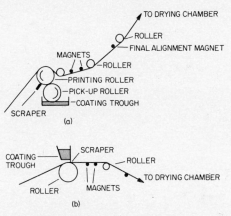

Fig. 49. Tape manufacture. (a) *Elements of the rotagravure coating process.* (b) *Trough and blade coating process*

89

As Fig. 49 indicates, there are two main coating methods: one is a rotogravure process like that used in the printing industry, and the other may be regarded as a casting process.

In the first process the coating is in a trough into which a printing

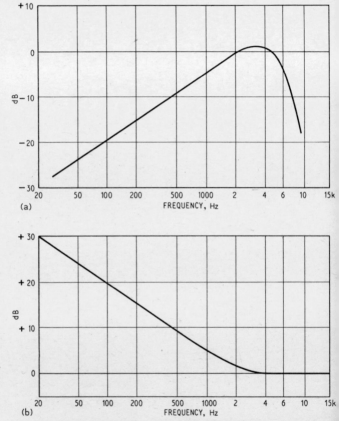

Fig. 50. Frequency response curves: (a) uncorrected response for tape at 19·05 cm/s (7½ i.p.s.); (b) C.C.I.R. replay curve

roller dips. This component is engraved with a pattern of spiral lines or dots; as it rotates a knife blade removes the surplus material, leaving small depressions (formed by the pattern) filled with the coating dope. While the dope is wet the tape passes one or two magnets which disturb the coating particles and ensure the required even dispersion in the dope. In the other process a slit in the coating trough allows dope to reach the tape, and surplus is removed by a scraper. The rest of the process is like the rotogravure method already described.

In coating materials development, emphasis has been on shape and uniformity of magnetic particles, and recent work has produced gamma ferric oxide, with particles exhibiting good acicularity (i.e. tending to be needle-shaped). New methods reduce particle porosity and promote freedom from dendrites—branching of the acicular crystals.

Generally, advances in performance are in respect of high-frequency response, signal-to-noise performance (especially at high frequencies) and output. Chromium dioxide tape is now widely available, and recently Philips have announced the use of acicular iron particles in tape coatings, although this innovation has yet to find commercial outlet. Unfortunately, many tape machines are not properly adjusted to exploit the virtues of new tapes, and some are entirely unsuitable.

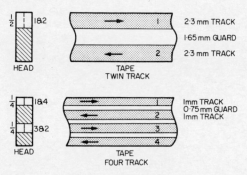

Fig. 51. Twin-track and four-track tape dimensions

What is the recording characteristic?

The uncorrected response for tape at 19·05 cm/s ($7\frac{1}{2}$ i.p.s.) is shown in Fig. 50. The response falls at the extremes of the range. For replay the equalisation does not provide the inverse of this curve: little correction is needed at high frequencies but some bass boost is required. Appropriate circuits are built into tape recorders and the electronic units used with decks.

The C.C.I.R. (European) characteristic is also shown in Fig. 50. The American N.A.R.T.B. curve is similar but some extra high-frequency attenuation is used on replay.

What are the track systems?

The two-track arrangement can be used for mono or stereo. However, a four-track arrangement (Fig. 51) is generally employed in machines for domestic hi-fi and is suitable for stereo or mono. Four

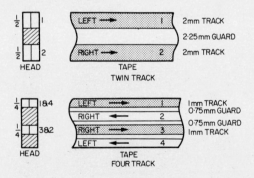

Fig. 52. Stereo tape track systems

tracks can of course be used for four-channel recordings. Track dimensions and the disposition of tracks relative to a head are shown in Fig. 52. Cassette tracks are dealt with separately.

How is tape added to an audio system?

If the machine is to be permanently associated with the hi-fi system, the obvious choice is a record/replay unit, essentially a complete tape recorder minus loudspeakers and probably also lacking power output stages. For hi-fi music purposes line outputs and a convenient selection of inputs (microphone, radio tuner, etc.) are all we need. Cassette units and open-spool machines are available in this form.

An alternative is the complete and transportable recorder. A high-quality recorder complete with output stages and, perhaps, small speakers for programme-checking purposes, can be disconnected from the hi-fi system and taken away when required for other activities. It should be understood, however, that a complete tape recorder is unlikely to provide the best basis for a hi-fi system; the output stages are not likely to function at a distortion level comparable with a specialised hi-fi amplifier and the output may not be adequate to drive insensitive speakers. A tape deck (the mechanical parts of a recorder) with separate record/replay circuits represents another approach, but the enthusiast is offered little choice of this type of equipment now that the complete record/replay unit is so widely accepted.

What is the cassette system?

It might be thought that the term 'cassette' could describe any device consisting of a tape in a housing, but in practice this word refers only to the compact cassette invented by Philips. The design, made freely available to manufacturers all over the world, was first used in small portable recorders—the equivalents of portable transistorised radios—but rapid development has ensured the entry of this device into the high fidelity field.

The cassette employs 3·81 mm ($\frac{1}{8}$ in.) tape and runs at 4·76 cm/s ($1\frac{7}{8}$ i.p.s.). It carries four tracks (two pairs for stereo), and a quadraphonic version with four tracks in each direction has been proposed. In stereo the two pairs of tracks are adjacent, not interlaced, so that a half-track mono cassette machine will play a stereo cassette as mono. The track arrangement is shown in Fig. 53.

Recent developments have led to more interest in the cassette at the hi-fi level, and this interest is being maintained as new tape materials come into use. Recent cassette machines have facilities for chromium dioxide tapes. At least as important is the improvement of the mechanical performance of cassettes and machines, and tape-jamming problems and speed fluctuations have been tackled. For example, the mechanical design of the cassette has been investigated by BASF and a 'Special Mechanics' version, running more smoothly and spooling the tape more neatly, has resulted.

Tape records, at one time issued only in the form of open-spool tapes (and otherwise but less correctly known as prerecorded tapes), are now released as cassettes and have proved popular despite their

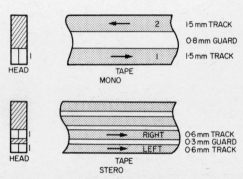

Fig. 53. Track system for cassettes. Head layout is shown

relatively high cost. These music cassettes still compare unfavourably with their disc counterparts, which are cheaper. Principal objections are restricted dynamic range associated with higher noise levels, restricted frequency range and higher distortion, as well as too-frequent tape drop-out effects. Improvement is slow but noticeable.

Typical performance features derived from test results on cassette systems are: frequency response 60–12,500 Hz within 5 dB; signal-to-noise ratio −42 dB through the record/replay circuits; wow and flutter 0·2%. Noise-reduction systems, of which the most important is the Dolby system, are essential in cassette machines for hi-fi use, and many modern units have the necessary circuits.

94

Apart from the widely used cassette, there is the inappropriately named tape 'cartridge', which is a housing containing an endless loop of 6·25 mm ($\frac{1}{4}$ in.) tape, lubricated for consistent performance. This device employs 90 m (300 ft) or more of tape running at 9·53 cm/s ($3\frac{3}{4}$ i.p.s.) and carrying eight tracks used as four stereo pairs. The cartridge has proved of little interest for hi-fi but is useful for background music applications in cars, boats and other mobile installations.

What are the principal noise-reduction systems?

Maintenance of the best possible signal-to-noise ratio is of outstanding importance in high fidelity sound reproduction and has become even more urgent with the growing complexity of audio systems, and in particular with the development of cassette recording and replay. Professionally, the most successful approach to the problem has been shown by the Dolby system, named after its inventor, Dr. Ray Dolby.

What is now called the Dolby A processor has been used for a considerable time by the recording studios in the production of their master tapes. The merits of the system have also been realised in simpler form in the Dolby B version for use in domestic equipment. This processor now appears in many cassette record/replay units priced at around £100 upwards and in a few open-spool machines. Commercial music cassettes, especially those by the Decca group, are Dolby processed.

The Dolby system is 'complementary', involving processing during production of a recording and balancing processing during replay. Dolby B processes signals to raise low-level, upper frequency components well above the noise threshold of the tape. On replay these signals are depressed, and with them the hiss is reduced. Fig. 54 show the processor in the record and replay path.

Several other noise-reduction systems have been devised: two Japanese systems find very limited acceptance in recent cassette equipment, and there is the Dynamic Noise Limiter (DNL) introduced by Philips. The latter is a replay-only system and therefore different in principle from Dolby. DNL can be regarded as a kind of automatic treble control. The lower the high-frequency level, the more the limiting is applied, thus reducing the noise that under such conditions tends to become obtrusive.

Both DNL and Dolby processors are made available in cassette machines and as separate 'black box' accessories. The application of the Dolby system has been spreading via licencees all over the world, and recently an integrated circuit version of Dolby B has been completed by Signetics of the U.S.A. It is to be expected that such devices will be incorporated in radio receivers and other equipment, although cassette tape reproduction, with its hiss problem, is still the prime candidate.

Which types of microphone are used?

Two basic types of microphone, pressure and velocity, are used with hi-fi equipment. In the pressure type, which includes moving-coil and crystal models, the diaphragm is open to sound on one side only, and the diaphragm movement is proportional to the instantaneous pressure developed in the sound wave.

In the velocity type, which includes popular ribbon microphones, the diaphragm is open on both sides and responds to the velocity of the air particles in the sound wave. The two basic principles may be combined in one microphone.

The polar response is of special interest to the amateur user. A pressure microphone is omnidirectional at low frequencies but becomes more directional as frequency increases. A velocity microphone is bidirectional, with a figure-of-eight polar characteristic, so that it picks up relatively little sound from the sides. A combination of the two characteristics will yield a highly directional microphone with a cardioid (heart-shaped) response, with low sensitivity to sounds arriving from the rear. A hypercardioid device has specially directional properties.

Polar responses are shown in Fig. 55. For outdoor recording a microphone can be made effectively directional, with a high ratio of wanted to unwanted sounds, if it is mounted on a parabolic reflector at the point of focus.

Moving-coil and ribbon microphones are low-impedance devices and popular models have matching transformers built into the housings. A high-impedance microphone is used with a fairly short

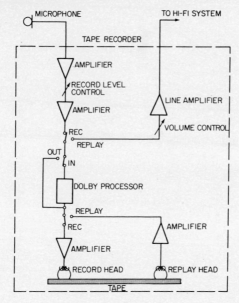

Fig. 54. Dolby processors incorporated in the record/replay system

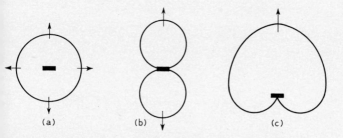

Fig. 55. Microphone polar response: (a) *non-directional or omnidirectional pressure operated;* (b) *bidirectional, figure-of-eight velocity operated;* (c) *cardioid or unidirectional*

cable, but a long cable can be used with a low-impedance microphone if a transformer is located at the amplifier end.

What accessories aid recording?

The hobbyist will wish to gain confidence in handling the tape. Editing blocks, adhesive tapes and other aids are available to the amateur tape editor and experimenter. These accessories, and such items as coloured leader tapes and jointing compounds, are supplied by tape manufacturers and other companies. Other aids include bulk erasers which handle entire spools of tape, and head defluxers which help to minimise noise levels in tape reproduction. Cassetted tape is not so readily edited, but the enthusiastic user can pull out the tape for splicing if necessary, and aids similar to those for open-spool tape have become available.

8

BUYING AND USING HI-FI

How important is planning?

Although personal taste and preference must influence the actual choice of equipment, it is essential to consider such matters as the space available, the output power needed, and the possibility of future extension of the system. These points can be considered when possible purchases are being short-listed and specifications studied; they are not necessarily directly linked to sound quality and can therefore be dealt with before auditions of equipment.

Those lacking deep knowledge of audio equipment are often advised to plan for a uniform level of quality through the system. Since this can help ensure that inadequacies at one point will not spoil the performance of the system as a whole, the advice is worth taking seriously. However, departures from such uniformity are possible for those with enough knowledge. Possibly the most important example is the association of very advanced disc equipment with a system for which such elaboration would not be a popular choice. It should be obvious that a pickup and turntable of superior quality are always beneficial, to some extent affecting audible results and, in any case, providing more precise operation and minimal record wear.

How should the budget be allocated?

Very many domestic stereo systems are in the medium-cost range, a system for disc reproduction only costing, say, £200–£250. At this level it is possible that the player (pickup and turntable), the amplifier and the pair of speakers would each claim about a third of the total, although for some rooms it would probably be better to allow a little more for the speakers and make small adjustments elsewhere. At the economy-class level of unit audio, a sum of £120 would be divided: 25% for the player (including cartridge), 45% for the speakers and 30% for the amplifier, assuming normal retail prices.

A feature of much more expensive systems is the high proportion of the total devoted to the disc equipment. A typical example for a large room is: £150 for the turntable and pickup (housed in a cabinet), £90–£100 for the amplifier, and about £150–£180 for the pair of free-standing speakers. The £100 amplifier becomes a £160 tuner-amplifier if f.m. radio is specified at the time of planning. The addition of a high-grade stereo cassette unit involves an extra £100, as a minimum. Allocation of the budget in this example would again be reflected in even more costly systems of professional type totalling £600 or more.

How are phasing and balance checked?

Loudspeakers for stereo must be in phase. With moving-coil speaker systems the following procedure should give unambiguous results. Place the two speakers close together and facing each other. If the phasing is wrong there will be a deficiency of bass in the sound. In that event it is only necessary to reverse the connections to one of the speakers, leaving the other speaker undisturbed, and then check that the bass has been restored.

It is then a simple matter to mark the speaker leads and terminals so that correct phasing is assured if, say, the installation has to be disturbed for some reason. Incorrect phasing can also be detected with the speakers in their normal positions, since this condition causes a vague stereo image. Reversal of connections as described should give a marked contrast and a much improved impression of detail in the stereo sound-stage.

Stereo balancing is done with the aid of a disc which contains a suitably simple sound, intended for reproduction mid-way between the speakers. The amplifier's balance control is adjusted to centralise the image. Special discs are available to aid the setting up of equipment and these provide the most reliable test signals. It should be remembered that some recordings display minor channel-balance faults and it may be desirable to use the amplifier control to shift the stereo image in the interest of realism.

How should discs be handled?

If modern equipment including a lightweight pickup is used it should be possible to keep discs in virtually new condition for many years. Cleanliness is essential and the recorded surfaces should not be touched with the fingers. Every effort should be made to keep dust away from both the discs and the turntable mat.

Record 'maintenance' is a problematical area of high fidelity. A few devices can safely be used to pick up dust from discs while they are played. However, cleaning methods that moisten the disc are generally suspect: it is only too easy to leave traces of moisture and dirt which harden to form noisy deposits in the path of the stylus tip. In general it is important to remove dirt from the groove but unwise to introduce substances into it.

The stylus should be gently cleaned with a small, soft brush. From time to time the tip of the stylus should be cleaned with alcohol. Avoid touching the stylus with the fingers.

How should discs be stored?

Discs should be stored in a dry atmosphere, preferably at living-room temperature but away from fires and radiators. A well designed cabinet will keep discs vertical and in compartments each holding about 20 discs of one size. It is helpful to provide extra dust protection by putting plastic bags over the record sleeves. Tapes should also be stored at a moderate temperature and away from strong magnetic fields, electric wiring and the like.

Should regular equipment checks be made?

The disc equipment, especially the turntable, should be regularly cleaned. A removable turntable mat can be washed; a turntable with a fixed mat can be covered with a rubber mat (suitable accessories are available). System interconnections and the mains lead and plug should be inspected occasionally, giving special attention to earth routes and the security of mains and speaker terminals. Terminations on pickup cartridges should be checked.

Occasional checks of pickup tracking, including bias correction, are advisable. For the utmost precision, the aids are a tracking weight gauge, a test disc and an alignment protractor for inspection of lateral tracking error. F.M. radio users should check aerial connections and the orientation of the dipole aerial. Users of tape equipment should not forget to clean tape heads. Cassette units can be treated with one of the special cassetted cleaning tapes.

Other maintenance tasks include the cleaning and lubrication of moving parts. Turntables should be dealt with in accordance with makers' instructions; maintenance routines vary and depend on details of design. For example, the main bearing may require greasing after a long period of use. The bearings of idler wheels require a drop of oil once a year; idler and turntable rim surfaces should be cleaned occasionally with methylated spirit on a clean, dust-free rag. Pickup arm bearings should not be lubricated.

INDEX

Teletext and Viewdata

Steve A. Money

Explains the concepts and technicalities of
information selection systems in a simple and
readable manner. Only a basic knowledge
of electronics is assumed and the book will be
of interest to viewers, service engineers
and students.

Although the book is devoted mainly to Ceefax,
Oracle and Prestel systems in the UK, the
information is also applicable to the systems
being developed in the USA and Europe,
particularly the French Antiope and
Tictac systems.

1979   160 pages   0 408 00378 2

Write now for a booklet on trade
and hobby books to

Newnes Technical Books
Borough Green, Sevenoaks, Kent TN15 8PH

Solid State Colour Television Circuits

G. R. Wilding

Provides information on colour television circuitry, including thyristor power supplies and line output stages, stabilised h.t. and l.t. supplies and over-voltage and current protection. Also covers delta-gun 110° tube convergence circuits and those necessary for the PIL tube.

This book will be extremely useful to the service engineer, student technician and amateur as a supplement to the service manuals of major British, European and Japanese receivers.

1976   200 pages   0 408 00228 X

Available from

Newnes Technical Books
Borough Green, Sevenoaks, Kent TN15 8PH

Practical
Electronics
Handbook

Ian Sinclair

A useful and carefully selected collection of
standard circuits, rules-of-thumb and design
data.

Covers passive and active components,
discrete component circuits and linear and
digital i.c.s.

Describes the operation and function of typical
circuits whilst keeping mathematics to a
minimum.

208 pages   216 x 138mm   0 408 00447 9

Newnes Technical Books
Borough Green, Sevenoaks, Kent TN15 8PH

Beginner's Guide to Computers

T F Fry

This book examines what computers can do and how they do it. After an introduction to the basic principles of their operation, the author describes the number systems which computers use and examines computer logic and the construction of logic gates as well as the workings of the central processing unit and of the various types of computer memory. Input and output devices are explained together with methods of storing and retrieving information.

1978   182 pages   0 408 00359 6

Newnes Technical Books
Borough Green, Sevenoaks, Kent TN15 8PH

Beginner's Guides

Other Beginner's Guides of related interest are

Beginner's Guide to Television   5th Edn.
Gordon J. King

1972   212 pages   0 408 00349 9

Beginner's Guide to Radio   8th Edn.
Gordon J. King

1977   240 pages   0 408 00275 1

Beginner's Guide to Tape Recording
Ian R. Sinclair

1978   176 pages   0 408 00330 8

Beginner's Guide to Integrated Circuits
Ian R. Sinclair

1977   192 pages   0 408 00278 6

Beginner's Guide to Transistors   2nd Edn.
Ian R. Sinclair and J. A. Reddihough

1975   160 pages   0 408 00374 X

Beginner's Guide to Audio
Ian R. Sinclair

1977   196 pages   0 408 00274 3

Beginner's Guide to Digital Electronics
Ian R. Sinclair

1980   160 pages   0 408 00449 5

All available from

Newnes Technical Books
Borough Green, Sevenoaks, Kent TN15 8PH

Write Your Own Programs
with

Introduction to Microcomputer Programming

Peter C. Sanderson

Package programs can be expensive and are
often unsuitable for your needs.

This practical guide tells you all you have to know
to write your own programs.

Describes BASIC, including common variants
and assembly languages of microcomputer
systems commonly available.

Covers the four assembly languages of the
microprocessors that form the basis of most
systems – Intel 8080, Motorola 6800, MCS 6502
and Zilog Z-80.

Includes practical hints on program testing
development and a glossary of terms.

1980   144 pages   0 408 00415 0

Newnes Technical Books
Borough Green, Sevenoaks, Kent TN15 8PH